D1179743

SMITHSONIAN INSTITUTION

BUREAU OF AMERICAN ETHNOLOGY

BULLETIN 199

# THE ETHNOARCHEOLOGY OF CROW VILLAGE, ALASKA

By WENDELL H. OSWALT and JAMES W. VANSTONE

U.S. GOVERNMENT PRINTING OFFICE

WASHINGTON : 1967

For sale by the Superintendent of Documents, U.S. Government Printing Office
Washington, D.C. 20402 - Price $1.75 (cloth)

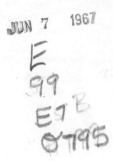
The Bulletins of the Bureau of American Ethnology began with the publication in 1887 of "Bibliography of the Eskimo Language," by James C. Pilling. The content of the Bulletins has been as broad as the contemporary interests of the field of anthropology, although mainly restricted in scope to the Americas.

With the publication of Bulletin 200, this series will end, its place being taken by a new series, *Smithsonian Contributions to Anthropology*, which was initiated in 1965 following the merging of the Bureau of American Ethnology and the Department of Anthropology of the U.S. National Museum into the Smithsonian Office of Anthropology. The new series provides not only for publication of scholarly studies of the American Indian but is worldwide in scope, reflecting the broadening activities of the Smithsonian Institution's anthropologists over the past few decades.

RICHARD B. WOODBURY
*Chairman*
*Smithsonian Office of Anthropology*

II

# PREFACE

In Arctic and subarctic America, where the aboriginal lifeways of Indians and Eskimos frequently have endured into the present century, historical archeology rarely has been of primary interest to either the ethnographer or the archeologist. In an area such as western Greenland, where there was sustained contact between Europeans and Eskimos, an exception is to be found. Northern Canadian historical archeology has been unsystematic, while in Alaska only along Prince William Sound (de Laguna, 1956; 1964), the Gulf of Alaska (Ackerman, 1965), and the lower Copper River (VanStone, 1955) have excavations been made at historic sites. In the Arctic and subarctic of America archeologists have yet to fathom the ramifications of many cultural continuities within the Christian Era, while the path of early man into the New World is still largely unknown. With fascinating problems such as these confronting them, it is not surprising that the archeologists have avoided sites containing tin cans, bottle glass, and crockery. Yet it is precisely these and other forms of trade goods in the context of a rapidly changing sociocultural setting that directed our attention to historical archeology in Alaska.

The geographical area of concern is the Kuskokwim River system of southwestern Alaska, where we had sampled sites in the 1950's. However, our interest was drawn to historical archeology in a roundabout manner. In 1953, Oswalt drifted down the Kuskokwim River in a small boat to collect tree-ring samples and to search for sites. One of the recently abandoned villages sampled was Crow Village, nearly 10 km. downstream from Aniak. While digging there, Oswalt was visited by Eskimos who recounted fragmentary ethnographic facts about the settlement and its occupants. When shown the artifacts recovered, the Eskimos were able to recall specific artifact uses and meanings. Thus, the collection served as an excellent prod to their memories. In 1954, Oswalt returned to Aniak to reconstruct riverine Eskimo ethnography, and with VanStone further excavations were made into the Crow Village midden. Although the digging period totaled only 3 weeks and frozen ground limited the depth of excavation, the artifacts recovered were numerous and diverse in form. In 1961 Oswalt analyzed a major source of ethnographic and historical data from the lower river in the unpublished writings of the Moravian Church missionary William Henry Weinland (Oswalt, 1963 b). Additionally, over the span of 10 years all of the published and many unpublished ethnographic and historical source materials for the region have been studied.

After the accumulated Kuskokwim data were assessed, a number of factors became apparent to guide future research along the river system. First, the sector from the river mouth to the upstream community of Kalskag had been studied in broad outline (Oswalt, 1963 a, 1963 b) and the overall shifts of ethnic groups through historic time plotted for the river system (Oswalt, 1962). Second, the two seasons of anthropological studies of Edward Hosley (1961) on the upper river were beginning to yield positive results for this, the least known locality. A third consideration was that the middle sector of the river had been investigated only in a superficial manner and was an area suitable for developing a number of interests. The emergent aim became to gather additional information about the population of the middle river from the time of historic contact until around 1900. The ideal would have been to reconstruct completely the aboriginal ethnographic scene through informants, but there was no potential for doing so because of the rapidly fading memories of the people. It therefore was decided to combine historical archeology with ethnographic reconstruction and the use of historical sources.

The excavation of the Crow Village site seemed a logical first step toward a more complete culture history of middle Kuskokwim River Eskimo and Indian life. The reasons for choosing to dig at Crow Village are diverse and worthy of mention. First, it was occupied in 1843 when L. A. Zagoskin visited there and was still inhabited after 1900. Thus, Crow Village could be expected to represent a segment of a period of rapid change, one which was increasingly difficult for informants to bring to mind. Second, from the test excavations of previous years the site was known to be productive. Third, the area was small enough to be excavated in a single summer. Finally, there was the availability of informants who either were born at Crow Village or had had intimate contact with the village and its inhabitants. The Crow Village excavation was begun in early June of 1963 and completed 5 weeks later. In retrospect, there were both advantages and disadvantages in selecting this site for the purpose conceived. It proved to contain less material than the midden tests had suggested, and no clearly separate levels representative of Russian and then American influences were established. Furthermore, individuals who had been capable informants 9 years earlier were either dead or approaching senility in 1963, a fact which made it difficult to obtain further information about the site and the recovered artifacts.

Historical archeology makes possible a realistic conjunction between written history, oral history, and traditional ethnography for more certain sociocultural reconstructions. Hopefully, the lines which divide scientific archeology from ethnography and history are largely those of methodology and not purpose. The combined approach is well established in the sphere of Near Eastern classical studies and is an increasingly important method of studying New World ethnic developments through time. In the study of primitive people it seems sound to begin by first excavating historic archeological sites. The comparative information available for the recent past is virtually always more complete than for the more distant past. Thus, it is logical to develop an archeological program in any particular geographical area by digging the recent sites and then working back in time to older sites. However, the overwhelming majority of archeologists compound their already staggering interpretive problems by being obsessed with antiquity. Thus many potentially useful sequences hang in uncertain limbo or are linked to history by frail suppositions and inferences. We hoped to avoid this pitfall through the kind of archeology we undertook. A specific contribution of the Crow Village data is that through them we may learn about the immediate effects of material change when the agents of change are from Western societies. This seems significant since it is innovations from the Western world that most often have led modern primitives in new directions. We hope that the Crow Village study will provide tangible results in this direction.

After having excavated Crow Village and analyzed the collection, we see additional sites that now have greater meaning. For example, some 50 km. upstream is a site, Kwigiumpainukamiut, which is contemporary with Crow Village and was occupied both by Eskimos and Indians (map 1). One end of the village was settled by Indians and the other by Eskimos, thereby providing an opportunity to study a situation of cultural contact in an archeological and quasi-historical framework. Furthermore, some 16 km. still farther up the river is a historic site of Indian occupancy. Finally, there is the old Russian trading center of Kolmakov Redoubt, whose excavation could provide a valuable baseline for the kinds of objects introduced into the area. The excavation of these archeological sites, together with historical and ethnographic supplements, would make possible a well-rounded study of the mutual impact of three peoples upon each other.

## ACKNOWLEDGMENTS

Excavations at the Crow Village site were supported by funds from the University of Alaska, the University of California (Los Angeles), the University of Toronto, and the Royal Ontario Museum. In the field, Mr. and Mrs. Jack Harrop of the Northern Commercial Company at Aniak were particularly helpful in making local arrangements for supplies and transportation. Mrs. Earl V. Clay, U.S. Commissioner in the same community, kindly made available vital statistics records that have been useful in determining the local movements of people in the middle Kuskokwim area. Mr. Anania Theodore of Aniak and Mr. Sam Phillips of Little Russian Mission provided valuable assistance in making the ethnographic reconstructions. Mr. William M. Oswalt provided general assistance while in the field, and we are pleased to acknowledge this aid.

We wish also to express our appreciation to Mr. Kenneth E. Kidd, formerly of the Royal Ontario Museum and currently on the faculty of Trent University, Peterborough, Ontario, for his interest in and support of the entire project. Other members of the museum staff who assisted the authors in various aspects of the artifact and bone analysis were Mr. Gerald Brett, Mr. Harold Burnham, and Dr. R. L. Peterson. The photographs were taken by the museum photographer, Mr. Lee Warren.

# CONTENTS

# ILLUSTRATIONS

## PLATES

(All plates follow p. 112.)

1. Chipped and ground stone tools.
2. Chipped and ground stone tools.
3. Wooden artifacts.
4. Wooden artifacts.
5. Wooden artifacts.
6. Wooden artifacts.
7. Wooden artifacts.
8. Wooden artifacts.
9. Wooden artifacts.
10. Bone, antler, and ivory artifacts, and locally made pottery.
11. Bark, wood, and plant fiber artifacts or raw material.
12. Metal, glass, and pottery artifacts.
13. Imported pottery and glass bottles.
14. Metal artifacts.
15. Wooden mask of a fox.
16. Human mask and human face of wood.

## TEXT FIGURES

## MAP

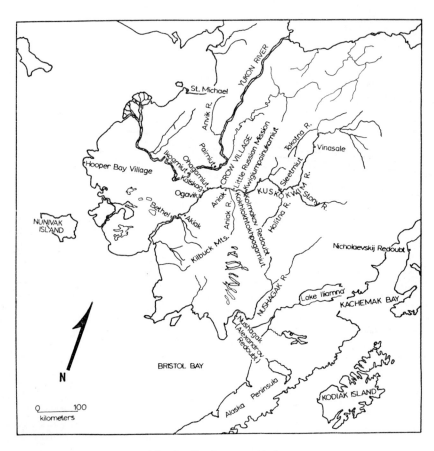

MAP 1.—Southwestern Alaska.

# THE ETHNOARCHEOLOGY OF CROW VILLAGE, ALASKA

## By W. H. Oswalt and J. W. VanStone

## CROW VILLAGE IN HISTORY

*Tulukaghogamiut*, as the site is termed in Eskimo, habitually has been rendered as "Crow Village" in English, but it would be more correct to translate the name as "Raven Village People." Throughout its recorded history this settlement was occupied by Eskimoan speakers of the Western Eskimo language stock. This linguistic grouping is separated into three major dialect clusters—Yuk, Cux and Suk (Hammerich, 1958); the Crow Village people spoke Yuk (Yuit, plural). This dialect was limited distributionally to an area extending north to the community of St. Michael and south to Bristol Bay and Iliamna Lake. The inland range of Yuk was to the village of Paimiut on the Yukon River and the vicinity of Crow Village on the Kuskokwim River. The Yuk-speaking Eskimos think of themselves as Yupik or "Real People," and some authors refer to the language by this designation. The Eskimos of the Kuskokwim River have the further local ethnic name of Kuskowagmiut, "Cough River People." The former residents of Crow Village could be termed as Yuk, Yuit, Yupik, Kuskowagmiut, or Tulukaghogamiut, depending on the context. Crow Village is the farthest inland aboriginal settlement whose residents spoke only Yuk. It is true that the village of Kwigiumpainukamiut was occupied by Eskimos, and it is farther up the Kuskokwim River than Crow Village. Kwigiumpainukamiut, however, was settled jointly by Eskimos and Athapaskan Indians of the Ingalik tribe and the Georgetown Ingalik subtribe. Hence, Yuk was not the only language of these villagers.

There are slight variations in the recorded Eskimo name for Crow Village, such as a transliteration from the Russian, Tulukagnag (Zagoskin, 1956, map), and early American period recordings of Toolooka-anahamute (Petroff, 1884, p. 16; map), Tuluka (Baker, 1906, p. 640), or Tulukagangamiut (Porter, 1893, p. 106). The designation "Crow Village" has been accepted in the present study because it is the locally prevailing English name for the site. It is likewise the

1

site's name on modern maps such as the Russian Mission quadrangle, 1950 edition, of the U.S. Geological Survey Topographical Reconnaissance Series.

The heart of Yupik country was along the central Bering Sea coast of Alaska. Here the people were oriented toward a maritime economy, in which the seal was most important. On the adjacent tundra some emphasis was attached to hunting caribou, and fishing for salmon was significant at the mouths of certain rivers and favored bays. The Yupik living inland on the tundra between the mouths of the Yukon and Kuskokwim Rivers subsisted mainly on whitefish, with caribou as a supplement. The Yupik penetration into the Yukon and Kuskokwim river systems occurred at some unknown point in prehistoric time when the people moved inland from the Bering Sea coast. It was the existing salmon fishing technology and the abundance of salmon locally which made it possible for them to exploit these rivers effectively. They had ascended the river some 280 km. from the sea at the time they founded Crow Village. It is possible also that some Yupik entered the Kuskokwim from the Yukon River drainage. Unlike other inland Eskimos, with the possible exception of those on the |upper Kobuk River, the people of Crow Village were following a way of life adapted to a riverine setting and to the northern forests.[1]

The first documented historical contacts on the Kuskokwim River between the Yupik and Europeans were made when a Russian party entered from the Bering Sea in 1818, but apparently they proceeded up the river only a relatively short distance (Tikhmenev, 1861, pp. 300–302). In 1830, according to Tikhmenev (1861, pp. 340–341), a group of Russian explorers, under Ivan F. Vasil'ev, ascended the Nushagak to its headwaters, and crossed a divide leading into the Kuskokwim River drainage.[2] The Vasil'ev party ascended the Kuskokwim and then traveled downstream to the river mouth and finally to Alexandrov Redoubt. The Vasil'ev journals of the trip have never been published, but these travelers must have passed Crow Village, if it existed at that time.

The first Russian trading establishment, built in 1832 at the Holitna and Kuskokwim Rivers junction, was within the area of Athapaskan Indian occupancy and near an aboriginal trading site that attracted Eskimos and Indians alike. The population of this immediate locality was so scattered, mobile, and sparse, that the purpose of the trading enterprise was not realized fully. This led to the abandonment of the original station and the founding of a second at the village of Kwigium-

---

[1] Much of the general information concerning the Kuskowagmiut in this chapter has been summarized from Oswalt, 1963 b.

[2] In previous publications Oswalt has incorrectly assumed that this explorer was Mikhail Nikolaevich Vasil'ev (e.g., Oswalt, 1963 b, p. 8).

painukamiut in 1833 (Zagoskin, 1956, p. 258). Once the Russians
had an inland trading center on the Kuskokwim, they hoped to develop
an overland route from St. Michael on the Bering Sea coast to
Nicholaevskij Redoubt on Cook Inlet. An exploratory trip origi-
nated at St. Michael and was led by Andrei Glazunov. In the winter
of 1833–34 the party descended the Anvik River drainage by dogsled
to the Yukon River and crossed the low divide to the Kuskokwim.
It is likely that they reached the river a short distance upstream from
Crow Village and then sledded on to the Stony River junction. Their
attempt to ascend this river to a Pacific Ocean drainage ended in
failure and near disaster, but they returned successfully to St. Michael.
The Glazunov party was near the Crow Village location on two
separate occasions, and it is possible that they stopped there, if the
village existed at that time. The travel journal, however, has never
been published in detail (see VanStone, 1959).

The second Russian trading center, Kwigiumpainukamiut, was
occupied only briefly before it was abandoned. The third station was
built diagonally across the Kuskokwim from Kwigiumpainukamiut
and was named Kolmakov Redoubt. From the time of its occupancy
in 1841 until the Russian-American Company withdrew from the
Kuskokwim in 1866, Kolmakov Redoubt was the major interior
trading establishment. The only early Russian of note to leave a
published record of his Kuskokwim travels was the naval officer
Lieut. Lavrentij A. Zagoskin, who visited the river in 1843 and 1844.
Zagoskin's was a trip of exploration and an effort to increase the
efficiency of the Russian-American Company trading operations.
He landed at St. Michael during July of 1842 but did not ascend the
Kuskokwim until November of 1843. On the 23d of November he
left the Yukon River settlement of Ikogmiut or Russian Mission for
Kolmakov Redoubt. On the 30th he stayed overnight at Crow
Village and arrived at Kolmakov in early December. He remained
at the redoubt, or in the vicinity, until early February of 1844, when
he returned to the Yukon drainage. In early April Zagoskin again
started toward the Kuskokwim and arrived there in the vicinity of
Kalskag. He apparently did not stop at Crow Village on this trip
to Kolmakov Redoubt (Zagoskin, 1956, pp. 206, 209–210, 211–212,
235–236, 255–256). In early May he made a trip by bidarka to the
upper Kuskokwim River as far as the vicinity of the Takotna River
junction, and at this point the narrative of his travels ends.

Zagoskin's account of the Eskimos and Indians is neither long nor
extremely detailed, but it is sufficiently complete to arrive at some
general understanding of aboriginal life among the Kuskokwim
peoples. He makes a few specific comments about Crow Village, but
what he notes about the Kuskokwim Yupik in general may be in-

terpreted as including the community of our primary interest. When he was at Crow Village in 1843 all of the people except one man and three women were attending a feast for the dead at Ohagamiut. At the time there were 90 residents living in 5 dwellings (Petroff, 1884, p. 37), and of this number 20 were Christians. Two of the Christian families had been baptized at Alexandrov Redoubt on the Nushagak River and only recently had moved to Crow Village. While Zagoskin was at the community, one of the old women gave him fish for dogfood, but the man stole his ax. In April of 1844, Zagoskin was at Kolmakov when two Crow Village natives who had been hunting caribou and beaver along the Aniak River came to trade, and after receiving tobacco plus a large metal pot, they returned home (Zagoskin, 1956, p. 267). These are Zagoskin's only specific textual references to the community and its people apart from references to the village location, comments which make it clear that the Crow Village site is the same settlement as that visited by Zagoskin.

The travel journal of Hieromonk Illarion, a Russian Orthodox Church missionary to western Alaska, dates from 1861 to 1868. In the summer of 1861 he went from St. Michael to the Yukon River, across the portage to Kalskag, and then on to Kolmakov Redoubt. The translated portions of the diary for this trip make no mention of a stop at Crow Village. He did, however, visit there on October 30, probably in the year 1863, and wrote the following diary entry (Documents Relative to the History of Alaska, vol. 2, p. 110):

We stopped over at the village of Tulukanagmute [Tuluka] because of a snow-storm, and I occupied myself with the natives, talking with them in their community hut. Among the subjects, we touched upon shamanism which they (although baptized) cannot yet entirely discard. When I told them how severely God punished and even exterminated the people for similar sins in ancient times, they replied, "You Russians have priests and doctors, but we have none. If any one happens to fall ill, who can help us except the shaman?" Similar replies I hear very often during my talks with the natives.

In the fall of 1866, when the purchase of Alaska by the United States was being negotiated, Prince Dimitrij Makŝutov, the Administrator-General of Russian America, traveled to St. Michael to arrange local details for the impending transfer. He decided to abandon Kolmakov Redoubt, and it was noted by Illarion (ibid., pp. 118, 121) that by November of 1867 the church property had been removed. Thus ends the formal record of Russian activities along the Kuskokwim River.

The meanings of Russian activities in the lives of Crow Village residents may be established only in the general framework of Russian expansion into interior Alaska (Tikhmenev, 1861) and from the Zagoskin and Illarion records. It is clear from these sources that the primary purpose of Russian penetration was to extend the fur trade northward. Trade items of Russian origin most probably were present on the river before the Russians arrived. In prehistoric and early historic times a flourishing trade existed across Bering Strait, and it is reasonable to assume that it affected the Kuskokwim. One of the responsibilities of Zagoskin was to determine how trade goods could be diverted to and controlled by Russian traders (Zagoskin, 1956, p. 48).

While the Eskimos appear to have been willing to seek and utilize Russian trade goods, they at first exhibited hostile feelings about the presence of the Russians along the river. Vasil'ev and his party in 1830 constantly guarded against unexpected attack, and in face-to-face relationships the people were hostile. Vasil'ev did, however, gain the cooperation of some prominent men (Tikhmenev, 1861, p. 341; Zagoskin, 1956, pp. 44–45, 273). With the establishment of the first trading cabin in Indian country in 1832, the central Kuskokwim Yupik gained the opportunity to receive trade goods more directly but without having the Russians in the immediate vicinity. It is significant also that the first trader, Semen Lukin, appears to have had cordial relationships with the people (Zagoskin, 1956, p. 262). When the first trading establishment was moved down the river to Kwigiumpainukamiut, the village containing both Eskimos and Indians, the transfer must have led to more intimate and direct contacts with the Crow Village residents. Not only was the post nearer, but at Kwigiumpainukamiut there were no doubt relatives of the Crow Village people. Finally, the transfer of trading activities to Kolmakov Redoubt stabilized the trading pattern. The number of Russians occupied in trading activities was small, and consequently they posed neither a social nor political threat to the Eskimos. The traders maintained control over desirable products, and these could be obtained through trapping activities. The Russian traders seem to have asked little more of the people. It would be incorrect to regard the Kuskokwim trading venture of the Russian-American Company as a thriving business enterprise. Clearly the area was on the fringe of Russian New World colonial holdings. Access from the Bering Sea coast redoubts was difficult, which made physical ties with administrative centers tenuous.

During the early American period the trading posts continued with many of the same characteristics as seen before. The Russian-American Company monopoly was replaced by its successor and lineal descendant, the Hutchinson, Kohl & Company. The old Russian trading stations, including Kolmakov, continued to function until at least 1885, even at times with Russian employees. Within a few years Hutchinson, Kohl & Company had reorganized as the Alaska Commercial Company, and its major point of redistribution moved to Bethel nearer the Kuskokwim River mouth. At about this time Kolmakov possibly was abandoned as a store, although it reopened temporarily from 1910 to 1914 during a gold stampede (Maddren, 1915, p. 308). Apparently there was never a store at Crow Village, but it is recorded in the U.S. Commissioner records at Aniak that Simon Kiogiack was a trader at "Crow Village" in 1919 and William Unalachluck in 1921. These Eskimos in all likelihood had in their homes a small stock of goods which they traded locally for the Alaska Commercial Company or an independent trader. For reasons cited later it seems likely that these trading activities did not take place at the Crow Village site but at a nearby locality. The same pattern, however, could well have existed at the site. Precisely where the major trading stations were along the central Kuskokwim River around the turn of the century cannot be stated with authority. Probably the most important store was at Ohagamiut. In any event the Crow Village Eskimos were able to obtain goods from a trader in the general area, but it is probable that supplies were neither diverse nor extremely plentiful.

The first census in which Crow Village reappears after the enumeration by Zagoskin is the Federal census of 1880. It is recorded that 59 individuals lived there (Petroff, 1884, p. 16). In the Federal census of 1890 the population is recorded as 17; 8 males and 9 females (Porter, 1893, p. 6). The village is not listed in subsequent decennial census reports.

No textual references are known to exist regarding Crow Village between the time of the Illarion comments and a remark made by the Moravian missionary William Henry Weinland. Weinland, while traveling up the Kuskokwim River in 1884 to select a site for a mission, records in his unpublished diary that on July 1st the party camped on an island near "Tvoluka-anahamut." In a list of the major villages along the central sector of the river he does not record Crow Village, but he wrote a note concerning the occurrence of other settlements which were deserted or consisted of only one or two dwellings. Presumably Crow Village would be in one of the latter categories (Weinland Coll., W. H. Weinland diary entries July 1, 7, 1884).

The period around the turn of the present century was recalled by informants who were familiar with the community while it still was occupied. One Eskimo, Anania Theodore, who was born along the Kuskokwim and who has lived at Aniak much of his adult life, stated that he visited Crow Village in 1901 or 1902 when there were about six resident families. Matthew Berezkin, a former Russian Orthodox priest, stopped here about 1906, and he recalled in 1956 that there were three resident families living on the site at the earlier date.

Mr. Berezkin said further that it was abandoned when he traveled down the river in 1912. By the latter date, he said, the old village was deserted and its former residents had moved downstream about 1 km., just below a bluff on the same side of the river. The reason the site had been abandoned, again according to Berezkin, was that a change in the river channel caused silt to be deposited in front of the village and made it difficult to land a boat there.

Another means for establishing the terminal date of occupancy has been to consult the files of the U.S. Commissioner at Aniak. The birth records available, for the period 1914 through 1942, were helpful since they include the year and place of birth of an individual as well as the parents' places of birth and ages at that time. These records also add an element of confusion since Crow Village is not distinguished from "New" Crow Village. Nonetheless, it is possible to make a few pertinent comments after discussing the records with informants. For example, one particular child was born at "New" Crow Village in 1914, while his father was born at "Old" Crow Village in 1887. Another man was born at "Old" Crow Village in 1893, and a woman was born there in 1887. This is slight but significant evidence to support the Berezkin statement that the old site was abandoned before 1912.

One Eskimo, Sam Phillips, or "Crow Village Sam" as he is better known, was born at the site in 1893, if his estimated age of 70 in 1963 is correct. The memories of his youth are neither systematic nor vivid, but he was able to recount certain facts concerning the settlement. He lived there until he was about 10 years of age and then moved to the new downriver settlement. According to him most of the people moved away from the site just after the *kanukpuk* or "big sickness," as the influenza epidemic of 1900–1901 is termed. Probably Sam's family relocated at this time too, since his age today and his age when he left the site are both approximations. This particular epidemic, according to a medical doctor stationed at Bethel during the time, claimed the lives of about half of the adults and all babies (Anderson, 1940, p. 198; Romig, 1901, pp. 33–34; Schwalbe, 1951, pp. 84–85).

Sam Phillips and Anania Theodore offered the following specific observations about the site when it was occupied. The abandoned settlement is located in a semicircular depression that is backed by a ridge on all sides that do not face the river. At present there are birch trees growing on the surrounding hillside, but when the site was occupied, the trees and brush purposely were cleared away in order to give a distinct view of the ridge. The clearing was a protective device enabling the residents to see anyone approaching from the land side, a route that would be followed only by unfriendly persons. Sam offered this description, but did not place a great deal of faith in its validity. Crow Village was so named because ravens have been attracted to the vicinity for a long time. They nest nearby and frequently are seen flying about the village. This was true when the site was occupied and was still true in 1963. Another tradition is about a spring forming a small stream that divided the village into two segments. The old people believed that if the spring were to go dry the salmon would cease to run in the river.

Aleš Hrdlička (1943, pp. 319–320) visited the Crow Village site in 1930 and described it as follows:

Reach Old Crow site, and greeted by cawing. See crows on trees back of the site—must be something favorable here for these birds. Water here shallow, boat anchored off. Get to bank over dark sticky mud from which it is hard to pull boots, and over willow brush. Site itself on a rather high irregular elevation, covered with rank grass, and full of smaller or bigger holes into which one falls again and again—as usual. After exploring find a few above-ground burials in the edge of the woods. Laborious to uncover skeletons, and these in poor condition. Secure barely parts of two and an adolescent skull.

Hrdlička reproduced a photograph of the site, in which it appears much the same as in 1963. Informants recalled that the burials obtained by him were taken from part way up the ridge on the upriver end of the site. With the description by Hrdlička end the known historical references to Crow Village.

## EXCAVATIONS

When first seen from the Kuskokwim River, the site appears as a grassy ridge some 14 m. above the river level. Scattered along the irregular surface are young birch trees, while behind the ridge on all flanks except the one facing the river is a steep hillside covered with large birches and a few spruce. Between the riverbank and the base of the ridge is a dense thicket, of alders and willows, which is up to 15 m. in width. Landing a boat in front of the site is difficult because the river becomes shallow very gradually toward the shore. The soft alluvium next to the bank on which the alders grow is interspersed with pools of standing water, and the thicket is impossible to penetrate with ease. There is every reason to accept informants' statements that the site was abandoned primarily because of this building bank. Toward the site beyond the alders is a low discontinuous bench with driftwood at its upper margin. The driftwood represents the height of spring floodwater. The luxuriant growth of bunchgrass on the site makes walking difficult, and scattered depressions in the grass are another obstacle. Once the site is reached, attention is attracted to one large and obvious depression. This is the outline of the cere-

monial structure or *kashgee* mentioned by Zagoskin, Illarion, and
informants (see fig. 7 for reconstruction). In the 3-meter pit is an
exuberant growth of alders in 1.5 m. of standing water. Just upstream from the *kashgee* are the remains of two adjoining house pits,
each with construction posts protruding above the sod layer. Downstream beyond these houses and the *kashgee* is a small house pit, and
in a slight draw still farther downstream are the remnants of cache
poles. Across the small streambed near the middle of the site the
first sign of former occupation to be seen on the upriver section is
four posts marking where a cache probably once had stood. A little
farther is another set of cache posts near the tunnel of a dwelling,
while beyond this house is still another house. A search along the
irregular brow of the ridge facing the river led to the discovery of
midden debris just downstream from the *kashgee* entrance. The
midden material was eroding out of the bank and was the first sector
of the site to be tested. In 1953 Oswalt dug into the face and recovered wooden artifacts and a few trade items, but the excavation in
1953 was limited to tests here and elsewhere over the site. In 1954
the authors excavated an adjacent midden section 5.4 by 9.1 m. to a
depth of up to 1.2 m., which represented the maximum thickness of
the cultural debris.

The purpose of the 1963 field season was to excavate the site as
fully as possible. The first step was to strip the sod layer from each
of the five house pits, their adjoining tunnels, and entryways when
these existed. An additional area of sod measuring 4.6 by 4.9 m. was
stripped from the brow of the ridge adjoining the 1954 excavation.
A second smaller midden was found in front of the two houses with
adjacent entryways (H-3, H-4), and here the sod was stripped from
an area measuring 1.8 by 5.5 m. An attempt was made to drain and
excavate the *kashgee;* however, it could be drained only partially
because of the depth of the water and the nature of the surrounding
slope. Excavating the houses and middens to their completion was
in itself a full-time task, and it is doubtful whether the *kashgee* could
have been excavated completely in the time available. It should
be added that the midden debris found in front of the *kashgee* most
probably represents a sample of materials to be found in this structure.

## HOUSES

Excavation of the houses posed no particular problems that are not
already familiar to archeologists who have worked in the Arctic or
subarctic. The usual difficulties surrounding the rate of thaw and
drainage after a rain were encountered. When we arrived at the site
on June 8, the 50-cm. layer of sod still was frozen partially. Thus it
was necessary to strip away the thawed upper sod and to repeat the

process a few days later for the lower sod. In general it was found that two individuals could remove the upper sod of one house a day. Then a 2- or 3-day interim was necessary for the thaw to penetrate the lower sod layer, and another day of labor was required to remove it. The debris between the sod and floor was removed in 2 or 3 days' time depending on house size and other conditions, while the floor of a house was excavated in about 2 days. The only problem encountered was with reference to the frozen ground in one section of a tunnel (H–3) that had not thawed by the time the other houses had been excavated. Another problem, that of draining rainwater from the house pits, necessitated the excavation of a complex series of ditches which consumed time and effort but yielded no artifact rewards.

Certain generalizations about the five houses at Crow Village are appropriate before discussing the details for each one in particular. First, it should be stated that all of the houses were occupied simultaneously during the period of early historic contact. Zagoskin in his population table (reproduced in Petroff, 1884, p. 37) records that there were five houses and 90 residents. He probably compiled these statistics while visiting the Kuskokwin River in late 1843 or early 1844. Thus, we are dealing with a cluster of contemporaneous residences. The similarities or differences which occurred in house construction potentially represent the range of technological knowledge available to all local housebuilders. This is not to say, however, that the houses were all built at exactly the same time.

In constructing the houses no effort was made to use stone although it was available at the nearby bluff and even on sections of the site proper. The builders, with a single exception, restricted themselves to the use of wood and natural features. In each instance an excavation, slightly larger than the proposed house, was made in the ground before the wood construction was begun. Thus all the houses were semisubterranean dwellings. In one case (H–1) the excavation was shallow, since bedrock protruded through the floor. The natural slope of the hillside at the rear of H–1, H–2, and H–5 was dug into so that the hill formed the rear walls. This mode of construction is not associated in any obvious manner with the absence of level ground upon which to build, but seems to be a culturally defined preference.

The species of wood employed in house construction were spruce and cottonwood. Spruce was utilized for all wall logs and uprights, while spruce and cottonwood were used for roof timbers. The roof beams in all but H–5 had disappeared. At the level of the roofs were recovered either sheets of birchbark or coils of birchbark; the latter no doubt had been flat originally. In one instance (H–5) the sheeting clearly was above the roof beams and served as a protective layer. It is very likely that, on the roofs of all the houses,

sod or dirt was placed on top of the birchbark sheets to keep them
from coiling and to form a more substantial protective cover. In
each house there was clear evidence that some of the construction
timbers had been removed prior to the collapse of the dwelling.
It should also be noted that cottonwood disintegrates rapidly after
it has been cut. Timbers from an abandoned house would provide a
ready supply of firewood or seasoned construction timbers. The
removal of these logs, or their disintegration, increased the difficulties
in determining certain details of house construction, particularly
with regard to roofs.

Tunnel entrances are common features of Eskimo dwellings, and
they occurred on the houses with one exception (H–1). The tunnels
of three houses (H–2, –4, –5) opened toward the riverbank, while one
(H–3) paralleled the bank in an upstream direction. The depths of
the tunnel floors varied from being essentially the same level as the
house floors (H–2, –4, –5) to beneath the floor level, thus forming a
cold trap (H–3). In each instance where a tunnel was present a log
or planks separated the inner tunnel entrance from the house floor,
and the tunnel did not protrude into the house. A series of parallel
horizontal logs or planks formed the tunnel sidewalls (H–3, –4, –5)
or else short vertical logs with horizontal retainers occurred (H–2).
Short, split, horizontal logs consistently were placed on top of the
tunnel wall logs and at right angles to these to form the tunnel roofs.
Contrary to the situation for the houses, the tunnels were not robbed
of logs prior to their collapse; it may be assumed that it was too
difficult to remove them for secondary use. Even though the tunnels
were in a good state of preservation and undisturbed by man after
the abandonment of the houses, it is probable that the sides were
compressed somewhat from pressure by the earth, particularly after
the roof logs decayed. Thus, the tunnels are probably somewhat
narrower than they were when the houses were occupied.

Of the four houses with tunnels, three had entry rooms at the outer
entrance to the tunnel. In each instance most of the logs had been
removed before the structures collapsed, and therefore only general
remarks may be made concerning their features. The entry room
for H–5 was rectangular with walls formed of split spruce logs or
poles. At the opening to the entry room, part of a doorway was
recovered which was similar to one found at the tunnel opening for
H–3. One entry room served two houses (H–3, –4), and it too was
rectangular, its only additional feature being that it contained an
ash layer in one corner.

In overall plan the houses ranged from virtually square (H–1, –3),
to square with one skewed corner (H–4), to rectangular with the
longer sides at right angles to the entrance (H–2, –5). The peripheral

horizontal base logs usually were hewn, with the exceptions of a rear wall log (H–1), two sidewall logs (H–2, –3), and one front wall log (H–5), all of which were unmodified along their longitudinal surface. In H–4 the base logs were hewn, while the verticals forming the outer front wall were split. When horizontal base logs occurred, there were occasional small poles driven into the ground next to the logs (H–1, –2, –5) which probably served as support posts to keep the horizontals in place. In one instance (H–3), the base log, or the vertical wall logs which formed the base and wall, were missing, while in the fronts of H–2 and H–3 vertical split wall logs apparently negated the need for base logs. On the floors of all the houses dried grass was found everywhere except in the center. Furthermore, sheets or coils of birchbark were scattered about the house floors. Near the center of each house a hearth was found. Each fireplace consisted of a wood ash concentration, but it was never surrounded by stones or clearly delineated in any manner. In the center of each floor there was a highly compressed layer which gave every sign of being a well trodden surface. Rarely was anything except beads recovered from this layer. In this context it should be pointed out that when a house roof was removed, fell in, or burned, the covering of sod would fall in and quantities of windblown silt would first be deposited along the walls. Grasses would flourish in the peripheral area, but the center of the house would be more exposed to seasonal thaw and would probably contain standing water. Therefore, organic artifacts left in the center of a house would be quite likely to decay.

The log arrangement within the houses varied widely. In one dwelling (H–3), where the most extensive postoccupancy log pilfering seems to have taken place, there were no logs which could be interpreted as representative of internal structural features. In the two rectangular dwellings (H–2, –5), only sidewall benches were present, while in two others (H–1, –4) benches occurred along the side as well as the back walls. A plank-covered bench was present in H–4, and in all likelihood planks covered the benches in H–2. When there were rear benches, lampstands were found at the front of the bench (H–1, –4).

Roof form is more difficult to reconstruct than any other feature of house construction, but again there is rather clear evidence of considerable variation. H–1 had the remains of vertical posts almost equidistant from the sidewalls, and H–3 originally had the same type of arrangement but was now missing one post. The four posts probably supported four horizontal beams on their tops, and short roof poles stretched from the beams to the sidewalls in all four directions. This is the typical four-post center type of roof construction.

H–5 had this roof form with modifications; here the rear posts were adjacent to the back wall while the forward pair were set into the house a short distance from the front wall. The original four-post center roof of H–3 was replaced later by a variation of the four-post center type with the placement of the four posts near, or in, the front and rear walls. There is no indication in H–2 that four vertical posts ever existed. Were they present originally, it would be expected that they would be found, since this structure has the best preserved interior. In this instance it is assumed that a flat roof existed, but this cannot be demonstrated empirically. At the same time there is no evidence concerning roof construction in H–4, but the arrangement of logs in the northwest corner suggests that the roof may have been cribbed.

One further comment concerning house roofs is worthwhile. The residents of the houses, particularly those in H–3 and H–4, must have worked on top of the roof, for artifacts were found in the lower sod layer. These were almost always inorganic, suggesting that if organic items were left on the roof they decayed before the time of the excavations.

## House 1

Before excavation, this house (fig. 1) appeared from the original ground surface to be older than the others; the wall outline was less distinct, the center of the depression was more irregular, there was less bunchgrass growing in the pit and very little standing water in it. Once the excavation was completed, however, it appeared from structural features that our initial estimate of its age was incorrect. Perhaps this is a worthwhile observation to make about age estimates based on surface appearances. The builders of this house made a shallow excavation for the forward area of the floor but dug into the steep hillside at the back of the foundation and utilized the hillside as the rear wall. Additionally, the ends of the sidewall logs at the rear of the house were embedded in the hill More hand-hewn construction logs were recovered here than in any other house, and in one front corner they were found stacked four high. In this southeast corner, it appeared from the height of the exterior sod that, originally, layers of sod probably were piled around the outside of the house front. The inference drawn from the abundance of hewn logs present is that the technological knowledge of how to square logs and the equipment necessary to do so were available to the builders, but this is less obviously the case with reference to the other structures. This dwelling did not have a tunnel such as was found attached to each of the other houses. Instead, in the wall facing the river, there was a gap that must have been an opening for a door. The outer wall construction

details suggest that here we have an attempt to build a log cabin but
without a detailed knowledge of cabin construction, since the front
corners were not mortised.   From the number of small vertical poles
placed along the inner front and sidewalls it would appear that these

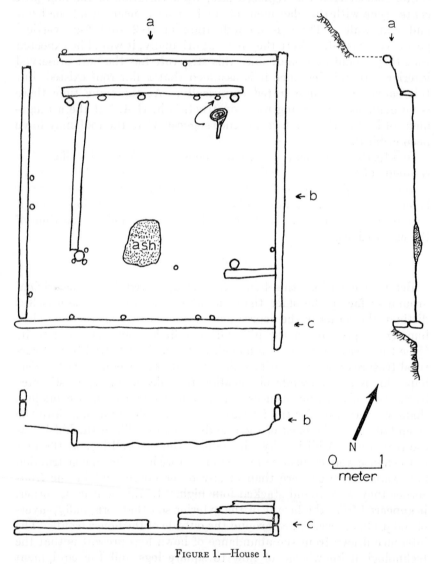

Figure 1.—House 1.

walls did not remain vertical as the builders had hoped, probably because the logs were stacked but not interlocked at the front corners.
The problem of sidewall stability probably was not as critical since
some balance would have been achieved there with the log ends em-

bedded into the hillside. At the rear of the house, in front of the bench, a stout split log was placed along the excavated surface. This log apparently was not sufficient to hold the ground behind it since three substantial vertical posts were embedded in front of the log to hold it in place. A wooden lampstand was similarly placed and served the same function as the posts but only secondarily. This stand was 60 cm. high and had been made by cutting a spruce burl horizontally across the middle. On the eastern side of the house there was probably a bench, but only one supporting log remained. The bench support and the absence of debris beneath where the bench would have been lead to this conclusion. The outer walls, the absence of an entry room or tunnel, and the presence of a doorway all suggest that this house had the outward appearance of a cabin. However, the roof construction was not similar to that of a cabin but was of the four-post center form. If these interpretations are correct, the structure represents a novel dwelling type.

## House 2

This was the smallest house at Crow Village as well as the one which contained the fewest artifacts and the thinnest layer of cultural debris on the floor (fig. 2). Like H–1, this too was assumed to be older than the houses beyond the draw. The reasons for the assumption were the same as for H–1, but again it is doubtful that they were valid. All indications are that H–2 was occupied for a shorter period than the other structures. It was built into the hillside, and the excavated area was used as part of the back wall. One unusual feature of this house was that a stone was placed beneath one of the horizontal bench supports, apparently in an effort to level the support. It was here that the only use of stone was observed in house construction. Another unusual feature was the use of extremely large heavy beams for supports beneath the benches. No reason for the use of such large logs is apparent. The only possible explanation is that they were cut and available. It is difficult also to understand why small poles were placed on the excavated surface at the northwest corner of the house and then construction logs placed on top. This may have been done as a leveling technique, but such an explanation does not seem adequate. No details of roof construction are available, but from the size of the structure it might have had a flat roof. The tunnel of this house was not unusual in any way, but it is noteworthy that no entry room was attached.

## House 3

As mentioned previously, this dwelling (fig. 3) had been rather thoroughly stripped of construction logs after its abandonment but before its collapse. The most striking feature was the depth of the floor debris in comparison with the debris in all the other houses, suggesting that it was occupied for a longer period of time or else more intensively. The floor layer was not everywhere continuous,

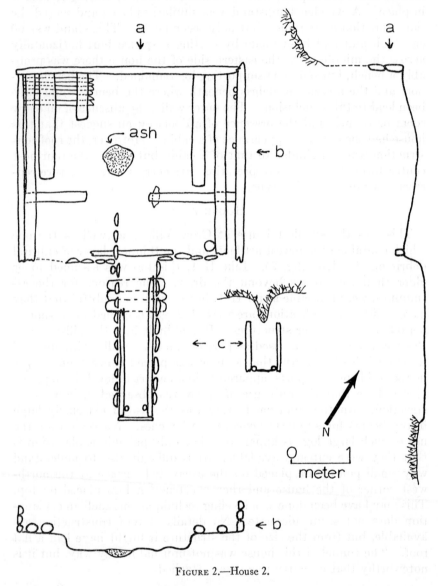

FIGURE 2.—House 2.

which leads to the assumption that the structure was abandoned temporarily about halfway through its course of occupancy. Embedded in the floor were the bases of three heavy posts which probably

represented three of the four posts necessary for four-post center roof
construction (see fig. 3).    Each of the posts had been cut off beneath
the upper level of the floor debris.    From this we would infer that the

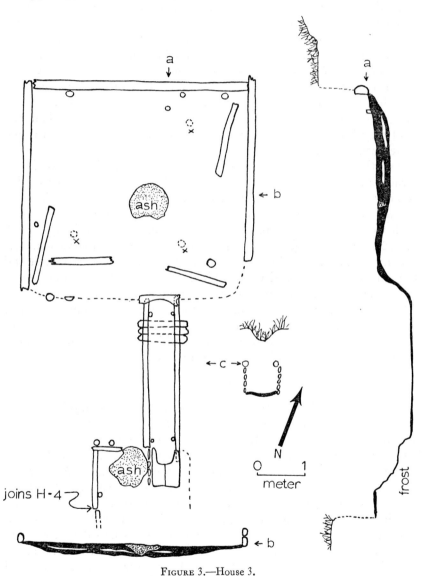

FIGURE 3.—House 3.

original house roof was of the typical four-post center form, but this
roof was removed, clean soil scattered about purposefully or acci-
dentally, and a second roof constructed.    The vertical logs for supporting the second roof were set near or in the front and rear walls.    These

posts are quite near the lateral walls and possibly made up a complex pitched roof or one that was cribbed.   Just beneath the sod layer was found a large quantity of charcoal, suggesting that the final roof had burned.   The base logs along the floor, however, were not burned. The occupational break for construction of a second roof was of brief duration, as evidenced by the continuity in imported pottery, window glass, and bead forms which were recovered throughout the floor.   The four sections of logs scattered about the house floor probably were left in their positions by the persons who had removed the other logs and do not represent any meaningful structural association.   In the present context it is notable that there was no evidence of benches. Had they been present it is likely that some indication of them would have been found.

The thickness of the occupation level, the two periods of roof construction, and the depth of the tunnel all suggest that this dwelling is older than any of the others at the site.   Elsewhere in Alaska deep tunnels forming a cold trap are chronologically earlier than tunnels with the floors at the same level as the house floor (Giddings, 1952, p. 112).   The tunnel in H–3 was in a fine state of preservation.   At the inner end a hewn sill marked the approach, while at the outer end the entrance was defined by two planks fitted together and cut away at one end to form an oval opening, probably at the ground level. At the outer entrance the tunnel opened on an entry room which was at the same level as the house floor.   The amount of ash in one corner of this room represents another hearth which may have been shared with occupants of the adjoining house (H–4).

## House 4

Before excavation the pit contained some 30 cm. of standing water, and numerous posts protruded through the sod.   This house (fig. 4) was in a better state of internal preservation than any of the others. The plank-covered bench was intact, except for frost heaving, which was contrary to the situation in all the other dwellings.   Around the bench support in the northwest segment of the house a metal band was found in place, and three similarly constructed bands were recovered nearby.   The one band still in place was bent around the sides of a horizontal support log and had a compressed S-shaped fold at each end.   It is assumed from the location of this specimen that it served to hold the bench planks in place.   There were, however, no nail holes in the metal for attachment to the log, indicating that the bands may have been bound to the planks.   Beneath this bench were found three bench plank supports.   Two were resting on their sides, while the third was upright beneath a rather thin section of plank (see pp. 36, 50 for descriptions of the clamps and bench plank

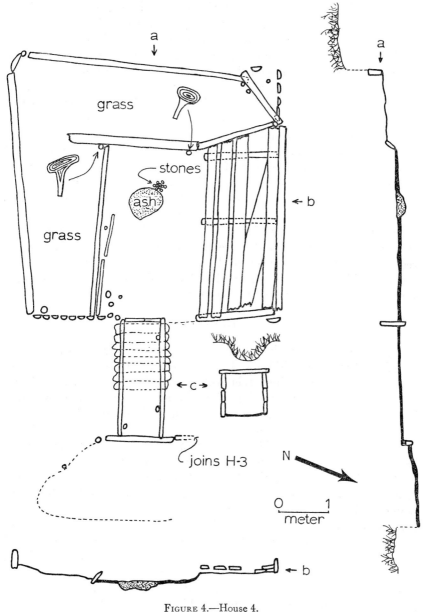

FIGURE 4.—House 4.

supports).   Neither the opposite sidewall bench nor the rear wall
bench were plank covered.   Furthermore, they gave no indication of
ever having been different from the way in which they were found.
Near the center of the floor adjacent to the ash layer was a cluster of

fire cracked stones which unquestionably had been used in cooking. Two lampstands were found in place just in front of the rear bench. One of these, like the lampstand in H–1, was made from a spruce burl, while the other was constructed from a piece of spruce root with a section of the trunk attached. At the front of the house along the southeastern wall the bases of all the split vertical wall posts were intact, while the poles along the adjoining wall, on the opposite side of the tunnel entrance, had been removed except for the corner post. The entrance to the tunnel was marked by two vertical planks over which it was necessary to step to enter the tunnel from the house. Likewise at the opposite end of the tunnel was a well-worn log sill. The entry room outline was obscure, but it was shared by the residents of H–3. The type of roof construction for this dwelling is problematical. The roof was not of the four-post center type nor a modification of this form. There is rather good evidence in the northwest corner that the roof was cribbed since a short horizontal log was found resting on the rear base log and on a short vertical post along the northern sidewall. It is conceivable that similar construction features were present in the remaining corners.

## House 5

The two dwellings which seem to have been occupied for the shortest length of time were H–2 and H–5 (fig. 5). Both had thin layers of floor debris and contained relatively few artifacts. H–5 had better preserved roof construction logs than did any other dwelling, which is its one important feature. Split roof beams of spruce and cottonwood were found along the southwestern segment of the house. The bases of these beams were outside the house proper, and the beams reached into the dwelling to the central floor area. Originally they were held up toward the center of the floor by two of the four posts employed in a modified four-post center roof construction. The benches were along the lateral walls and were covered with a heavier layer of grass than was found on the benches of the other houses. Indications are that these benches were never plank covered. The log-lined tunnel had a floor which was at a slightly lower level than the house floor, while the division between the house and the inner extent of the tunnel was marked by the front wall base log. The tunnel entry room was rectangular in outline, and like the house it unquestionably had been robbed of logs prior to its collapse. The one significant feature of entry room construction which could be discerned was that the entrance to this structure was marked by split planks with an oval hole cut into them; one of these planks was recovered.

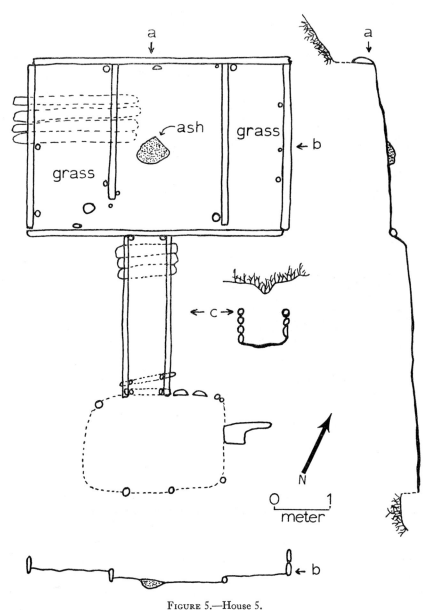

FIGURE 5.—House 5.

## CACHES AND CABIN

The remains of three different sets of vertical posts were located on the unexcavated surface of the site. These posts extended from about half a meter to a meter above the sod layer. They were

TABLE 1.—*House construction features*

| Feature | House No. | | | | |
|---|---|---|---|---|---|
| | 1 | 2 | 3 | 4 | 5 |
| Excavated foundation | X | X | X | X | X |
| Ground slope served as a rear wall | X | X | | | X |
| Spruce wall logs or poles | X | X | X | X | X |
| Spruce or cottonwood roof beams | X | X | X | X | X |
| Birchbark sheets or coils at fallen roof level | X | X | X | X | X |
| Logs removed before collapse of the house | X | X | X | X | X |
| Tunnel | | X | X | X | X |
|     Shallow floor | | X | | X | X |
|     Deep floor | | | X | | |
|     Wall logs horizontal | | | X | X | X |
|     Wall logs vertical | | X | | | |
|     Short split tunnel roof logs | | X | X | X | X |
| Tunnel entry room | | | X | X | X |
| House: | | | | | |
|     Dimensions virtually square | X | | X | X | |
|     Dimensions rectangular | | X | | | X |
|     Outer wall base logs hewn or split | | | | X | |
|     Outer wall base logs hewn or unprepared | X | X | X | | X |
|     Vertical outer wall logs along front of house | | X | (?) | X | |
|     Grass over most of the floor surface | X | X | X | X | X |
|     Birchbark sheets or rolls on the floor | X | X | X | X | X |
|     Benches: | | | | | |
|         Sidewall | | X | | | X |
|         Side and back walls | X | | | X | |
|         Plank covered benches | | X | | X | |
|     Lampstand in front of rear bench | X | | | X | |
| Roof: | | | | | |
|     Four post center | X | | X (1) | | |
|     Modified four post center roof | | | X (2) | | X |
|     Flat roof? | | X | | | |
|     Cribbed roof? | | | | X | |

always in groups of four and in rectangular arrangements. These post arrangements were the foundations for caches which were erected on platforms above the posts. One set of posts, in a draw at the downriver end of the site, was thought initially to have been a house. However, excavation of the area to a depth of 60 cm. clearly revealed that the ground beneath the posts was sterile and had not been disturbed by the builders of the cache. Another set of cache posts posed a different kind of problem. These were located downstream from the side of H–2, where an excavation was made beneath the posts (Test 3) and a few artifacts were recovered, none of which was in a defined cultural layer. Undisturbed soil was found about 30 cm. beneath the sod. Oswalt was convinced that the logs represented the corners of a cache, while the two horizontal logs on the ground were fallen supports for the cache. VanStone considered that this could have been a cabin that was almost completely removed after it was abandoned. In support of VanStone's conclusion is the statement by Sam Phillips, who lived on the site as a boy, that a cabin once had stood at or near this particular location. This cabin must have been removed, as VanStone assumed, but there is no satisfactory explanation for the vertical post if this was indeed the location of the cabin. We may conclude that a cabin existed toward the end of the site's occupancy, judging from the informant's statement, but whether or not it was at this particular spot remains conjectural. The only other cache post remains were near the tunnel entrance to H–2, and it must have been a relatively small cache. Other caches probably existed on the site judging from the number of rotting logs on the ground and the occurrence of isolated posts such as were found in the slight draw between the two segments of the site.

## KASHGEE

As mentioned earlier, the *kashgee* was not excavated because of the problem of draining the water out of the pit and the limited amount of time available for the excavation. The depression measured about 7.6 m. wide, 5.8 m. long, and had a maximum depth from the rim of 3 m. A test excavation in the downriver corners indicated that heavy vertical posts probably were used in the wall construction. All of these posts were charred at the top, leading to the conclusion that the *kashgee* probably had burned. Surprisingly, informants were unable to confirm this conclusion. The *kashgee* entrance faced the river, but from surface indications it could not be established whether it had a short tunnel or simply a wide entry room leading directly into the structure. Statements by informants were to the effect that a tunnel connected the *kashgee* with an entry room.

## MIDDENS

In 1953 and 1954, a 5.4-m. by 9.1-m. section of the midden in front of the *kashgee* was excavated. In 1963, digging was continued into this midden deposit with the further excavation of an area 4.6 by 4.9 m. These excavations were jointly termed test 1 (T–1). During the 1963 field season it was observed that there was a slight rise in front of the joint entry room to houses 3 and 4. Sampling this area revealed that here, too, was a midden deposit, and it was excavated fully (T–2). The only other test cut of any note was made at the cache or cabin location (T–3).

At Crow Village there was a differential potential for the recovery of midden debris associated with any specific house. H–1 was located very near the riverbank, and it is highly likely that the residents threw their trash over the bank. H–2 was set farther back from the bank, but there was no sign of a midden in front of it, and again it is assumed that the residents threw their trash over the riverbank. This situation might have been anticipated considering the very thin layer of cultural debris found on the floor of this dwelling. The generalization made for H–2 may be applied to H–5 since the same situation existed here. H–3 and H–4, however, were much farther from the riverbank, and the residents carried their trash only a short distance toward the river before dropping it. This was the only midden (T–2) located in association with the houses. It measured 3.0 by 6.1 m., and the cultural debris ranged in thickness from 80 cm. nearest the entrance of the houses to a few centimeters at the front of the deposit. The midden was not consolidated but consisted of leached organic material, silt, and scattered artifacts. The scarcity of artifacts and the likelihood that they were all deposited over a comparatively brief period of time led to the analysis of these specimens as a unit.

The *kashgee* residents carried their trash farther than the residents of any of the houses and threw it over the riverbank. Extensive testing from the *kashgee* entrance to the riverbank demonstrated that very little was dropped between these two points. At the time the *kashgee* occupants began to deposit their trash along the riverbank the dropoff was about 4.6 m. farther back than it was at the time of the excavations. The T–1 debris consisted primarily of wood chips. These were recovered throughout the midden and were more concentrated in some areas than others. When the abundance of wood chips decreased, the debris consisted of discontinuous lenses of silt, and concentrations of salmonberry seeds. The latter represented decaying human feces. The thickness of this deposit ranged from a few centimeters toward the *kashgee*, to 1.2 m. at the brow of the ridge, to sterile soil where the bank fell off sharply. From the 1953 and 1954 excavations in this midden, it was established that the artifacts recovered were of the same types throughout the depth of the deposit. Therefore the entire midden collection from this excavation (T–1) has been treated as a unit.

Scattered about the site but particularly at the downriver sector were artificial pits dug into the ground. These were up to 2 m. in depth and as much as 1 meter across. These were the remains of pits for storing fish, and each was unlined. At the center of the back wall of H–3 just beyond the structure was located a small birchbark lined cache pit which was excavated. This pit was 50 cm. across and approximately 40 cm. in depth. Along the inner facing of the birchbark lining small sticks had been stuck into the ground to keep the birchbark from falling into the hole. Nothing was recovered from this or any of the other ground caches.

# COLLECTIONS

In this section the artifacts from Crow Village are described under the major headings of locally manufactured goods and imported manufactured goods. Further subdivisions under each of these headings are according to the material used in the manufacture of the artifacts. The approach is largely descriptive, and no exhaustive comparative analysis is attempted. An analysis of the trade goods is found in the discussion of continuity and innovation, pp. 68–77.

## LOCALLY MANUFACTURED GOODS

Under this heading are included all artifacts manufactured locally by Eskimos irrespective of whether or not they are traditional Eskimo forms. Thus this section includes descriptions of artifacts made from materials unknown to precontact Eskimos as well as forms that were the direct product of the contact situation.

### CHIPPED STONE

The items included under Chipped Stone are chipped predominantly although some show additional stoneworking techniques. In most instances the working edges are chipped, and other manufacturing techniques are of secondary importance in the form and function of the artifact. It is probable that many of the chipped stone artifacts, particularly those of slate and basaltic material, are unfinished implements which would, in the process of their manufacture, have been finished by grinding and polishing. It seems worth while, however, to consider them here in order to emphasize the wide range of manufacturing techniques available to the 19th-century Eskimos at Crow Village.

*Hammerstones* must have played an important part in tool manufacturing at Crow Village, and the 13 recognizable specimens of this form vary widely in size and care taken in manufacture. Nine implements are roughly flaked basaltic cores which either have been blunted at one end to form a hammering surface or else have been shaped to fit the hand and show indications of their use on a flat surface. One of the latter, in addition to having been grossly shaped by flaking, also has been carefully pecked on the faces that would be grasped by the hand. Of the four more carefully made specimens, all of basaltic material, one is extremely large and heavy, 15 cm. in length, and has large areas of unworked surface. The working surface, however, has been chipped carefully, and there is evidence of considerable use. The remaining three specimens are chipped carefully and have well defined and skillfully prepared working surfaces (pl. 1, *j*).

A single *arrow point* of blue chert is stemless with some attempt at basal thinning and uneven flaking over the entire surface (pl. 1, *f*). The general appearance of this artifact suggests greater antiquity than that of the balance of the Crow Village lithic assemblage, and we suspect it may have been picked up by hunters along one of the ridges in back of the site.

Five implements are identified as blanks for *end blades;* all are made of slate and have been worked roughly into blade form—perhaps to be used ultimately as lance or man's knife blades. One specimen appears to be finished except for grinding the edges (pl. 1, *k*), while the others, as represented in plate 1, *c*, are relatively crude.

Three probable *ulu blade blanks* are of slate and are relatively small with convex cutting edges; furthermore, each is tangless and roughly flat across the top. The tapered and abraded upper edge of one specimen (pl. 1, *g*) suggests that it was cut with a stone saw.

In addition to the blade blanks for identifiable implements mentioned previously, there are 13 roughly chipped slate and basaltic fragments that appear to be blade blanks. All are thin in cross section, vary in length from 3 to 9 cm., and presumably would eventually have been made into finished blades or scrapers.

The single *net sinker* is simply a large, broken, basaltic beach pebble crudely notched on opposite sides for lashing. Carefully finished bone or antler net sinkers are not uncommon in the Crow Village collection, but the single stone specimen suggests that this particular form was rarely used.

Seven roughly made implements are identified as *boulder-chip scrapers.* All are made from flat ovate sections of basalt. Three were struck from beach-worn pebbles, while four have been struck from the sides of larger cores (pl. 1, *n*). This type of tool has been described by de Laguna (1934, pp. 60–61) as a boulder chip and by Rainey (1939, p. 360) as a "tci-tho."

Perhaps the most interesting category of chipped stone implements is the scrapers. *Side scrapers* of flinty material include one relatively large specimen with a carefully prepared working edge; this scraper probably was used unhafted (pl. 1, *e*). The remaining seven examples are crude flakes retouched on one or more edges. Two additional fragments of quartz have steep carefully prepared working edges (pl. 1, *i*). These may be hafted snub-nosed scrapers. *End scrapers* are not so readily recognizable, and there is some doubt about the use of the artifacts so identified. Six implements are regarded as hafted end scraper blades. Two are of blue chert with steep working edges (pl. 1, *h*). Three basalt samples are similarly shaped but larger (pl. 1, *d*). A single end scraper is of soft sandy schist, thin in cross section with a wide flaring working edge (pl. 1, *a*). One chert im-

plement has been identified as an unhafted end scraper (pl. 1, *b*). It
has a steep crudely fashioned working edge, and the distal end has
been reworked to a point as if for use as a gouge.

In addition to the identifiable artifacts, there are eight unidentifiable fragments characterized by chipping. All except a single
quartz fragment are made of basaltic material.

## GROUND STONE

Objects of ground stone form the second largest category of artifacts in the collection, but the significance of this fact is obviated
somewhat because a relatively small number of types are represented.
The most abundant artifacts in this category are *whetstones*, of which
there are 101 specimens. These have been divided into three types
based largely on the nature of the stone from which they have been
made. Those specimens belonging to type 1, of which there are 70,
are made of a relatively soft material ranging from coarse-grained
sandstone to a very fine grained sandy schist. Not a single example
of this type can be said definitely to be complete. In fact, the number of individual artifacts in this category may have been increased
by the tendency of the coarser-grained whetstones to exfoliate.
Many of the smallest fragments could be exfoliations from larger
implements. A wide range in size is represented. Four whetstones
in excess of 20 cm. in length and 10 cm. in width were discarded in
the field, while a number in the collection measure more than 15 cm.
in length. The smallest fragments are 2 to 4 cm. in length. All of
the type 1 specimens have at least two flat surfaces showing various
degrees of use. In most cases the unbroken edges of the whetstones
have been roughly worked, but only five can be said to be well shaped
(pl. 1, *l*, *m*, *o*). The illustrated specimens indicate the better made
examples.

Whetstones of type 2 number 19, but only 1 appears to be complete.
They have been shaped from relatively hard materials such as basalt
and silicified slate. They tend to be smaller than the whetstones
of type 1, the largest fragment being 11 cm. in length and most much
smaller. All specimens show wear on at least one surface; the best
examples are worked to a rectangular form and show wear on four
surfaces (pl. 1, *p*, *r*).

Type 3 whetstones are beach-worn pebbles that had been picked
up and used as sharpening stones. There are 12 of these, 3 of which
are complete. All show some wear on at least one surface, and the
illustrated specimen shows considerable wear on four surfaces (pl. 1,
*q*). Nine implements are of a hard stone similar to type 2, while three
are of a soft material like those in type 1.

A characteristic of whetstones in the Crow Village collection is that some specimens show indications of a secondary use. Two of the largest in type 1 have been used secondarily as hammerstones. The truly secondary nature of this use is indicated by the fact that the pits made by hammering occur on the worn surfaces. Two small fragments, one belonging to type 2 and the other to type 3, have small drilled holes about 2 mm. in depth, presumably indicating their use as drill bearings. Nine whetstones, six from type 1 and three from type 2, have deep, narrow striations on their worn surfaces which are probably the result of their use as sharpeners of steel needles (pl. 1, *l*). On three of these implements the striations are as much as 1 mm. in width, which would seem to suggest a heavy sailmaker's needle. This indication of the use of whetstones as needle sharpeners is of particular significance because no needles were found. Strictly speaking, it may not be completely true that such a use for whetstones was a secondary one. All of the striations, however, occur on worn surfaces of specimens and in most cases are relatively sharp and clear.

Seven artifacts served as blades for *end hafted skin scrapers*. Each is of soft sandstone, and of the four reasonably complete specimens, two have straight sides and are crudely fashioned except for the working edge which is V-shaped in cross section (pl. 2, *p*). A single scraper, also crude except for the working edge, is somewhat larger than the others and tapers toward the proximal end (pl. 2, *c*). The fourth complete specimen is double bladed with a roughened area between the two working edges (pl. 2, *d*). If this implement is indeed a scraper blade, it is difficult to imagine how it was hafted. At first glance the roughened area between the two working edges suggests hafting as a planing adz. However, a more likely explanation in our opinion is that one working edge was made first and, after considerable use, the other edge was made and the blade rehafted.

At least two writers have commented on the difficulty of determining whether small blades similar to those described above were used as planing adz blades or as skin scrapers (de Laguna, 1947, p. 186; Oswalt, 1952, pp. 57–58, 61). Oswalt remarks that "the only certain distinction between the small adz blades and scraper blades is that the former would not be made of soft material; the latter, however, might be made of either hard or soft stone" (1952, p. 58). Since all of the Crow Village specimens are of soft stone, they have been described as scraper blades, although at least two specimens might otherwise have been referred to as planing adz blades.

While whetstones presumably were used to sharpen previously existing blade edges, a single artifact has been identified as a *grinding stone* that would have been employed in the abrasion process during tool manufacture. This specimen is made of basaltic material and has either been pecked to a round shape or has achieved its form as a result of use (pl. 2, *j*).

The 10 slate *end blade* fragments in the Crow Village collection have finely ground surfaces and bilateral cutting edges. Seven are blade tips, two are basal fragments, and a single section is from the center of a blade. All of the specimens are characterized by a hollow-ground groove, apparently running parallel to the entire length of the blade since it is noticeable even in the basal fragments. Little can be said about the proximal ends of these implements except that the two basal fragments narrow to a flat base (pl. 2, *g*, *h*).

*Ulu blades* of slate include 4 complete specimens and 17 recognizable fragments. With regard to the shape of these implements, the only consistent element is the convex outline of the cutting edge. There is some degree of variability in this convexity, but the majority of the blades have a semilunar shape. Of the four complete specimens, two have tangs: one symmetrical (pl. 2, *e*) and the other irregular (pl. 2, *f*). One blade has no tang and is nearly flat across the top (pl. 2, *i*), while the fourth is rounded at the proximal end (pl. 2, *l*). None of the fragments is complete enough to indicate the presence or absence of a tang. Grooving on two of the fragments probably was accomplished with a stone saw.

Four fragmentary bladelike implements tentatively are identified as *stone saws*. All are made of abrasive material and are comparable in shape to skin scraper blades except for being somewhat larger and having working edges that are more bluntly V-shaped (pl. 2, *m*). Two specimens have striations along the working edge and parallel to it, a characteristic which seems to suggest their use with a sawlike movement.

Two fragments of *splitting adz blades* were recovered, but neither is complete enough to provide much information about the shape of these implements. One fragment is the distal end of what must have been a sizable adz (pl. 2, *k*). This heavy blade, which is thicker than it is wide, would have been lashed directly to an elbow or T-shaped handle and presumably would have been used for rough work such as chopping down trees and splitting logs. This basalt specimen appears to have been shaped by pecking, with only the concave cutting edge ground and polished. The second fragment is apparently from along the back of an implement and would be unrecognizable as an adz blade fragment except that a lashing knob is present.

Although there are only five examples in the collection, and only two of them are complete, the *planing adz blades* conform to two distinct types. Type 1, represented by a single complete specimen and three sizable fragments, is large and presumably was fashioned by primary flaking with only the cutting edge being finely polished. This type, which has straight sides and is flat across the top, probably would have been hafted directly to a shouldered handle (pl. 2, *a*). The complete specimen of this type and two of the fragments are of basaltic material, while the third fragment is of a more fine-grained greenish stone like jadeite. The second type, represented by a single complete specimen, also is crude except for the working edge but is much smaller and tapers toward the distal end (pl. 2, *b*). Such a blade presumably was fashioned for hafting in a socketed or bedded adz head, although no such heads were recovered. The type 2 blade closely resembles a previously described skin scraper blade (pl. 2, *c*) but has been classified as a planing adz blade because of its manufacture from a hard basaltic material.

A large, irregularly shaped, sandstone boulder with a shallow, carefully rounded and polished depression on one side has been identified as a *paint mortar* or pigment grinder even though there are few indications of use. The boulder itself is approximately 21 by 14 cm., while the depression, which is located to one side of the stone, is 6.5 cm. in diameter. The round depression is somewhat darker in color than the rest of the stone, and there are slight brown stains around its rim. Another possible identification for this specimen would be as a tobacco grinder.

A large fragment of a well-made *stone dish* is of basaltic material which has been carefully pecked on both the inside and out. This dish, which appears to be about three-quarters complete, was approximately 23 cm. in diameter and elliptically shaped. The rim, which is flat, is less well finished than the rest of the vessel and has a definite outward slope on two sides. A third side, which presumably resembles a missing fourth, is perpendicular and has no rim.

Perhaps the most unexpected manufactures of stone in the collection are two fragments of *stone lamps*. Since stone lamps never before have been reported from the Kuskokwim River region, it is worth considering these specimens in some detail. The largest fragment is of very coarse-grained sandstone and has been constructed by means of crude chipping and pecking. The complete lamp must have been extremely large since this fragment contains a rim segment 22 cm. in length without any indication of the shape of the complete object. We would be inclined to think that this object might be part of a large dish except that definite traces of a burned organic substance are to be found on the inside. Since there is no indication of burning on the outside surface of the specimen, its use as a cooking container is ruled out. The second lamp fragment, also of a relatively coarse-grained material, is much smaller and better made. The distinguishing features of this fragment are a wide, flat, upper rim, a shallow bowl,

what was probably an evenly rounded exterior, and a convex bottom
(pl. 2, *o*). This type of lamp, as pointed out by Hough (1898, p. 102,
pl. 20), is typical of Kodiak Island. Heizer also notes that Hrdlička
collected two lamps of this type from living Koniag, "and there is
every reason to believe that this was the type in use on Kodiak at
the opening of the historic period" (Heizer, 1956, p. 33, pl. 26, *c*).
Roughly similar lamps are illustrated by de Laguna (1934, pl. 24,
*1*; 1956, pl. 24, *4*) from Kachemak Bay and Prince William Sound.

Since pottery lamps were well established throughout the Kuskokwim River region and since stone lamps have not been reported
previously, it seems possible that the examples described from Crow
Village are not indigenous to the site but were traded into the area.
The large, crudely made fragment, though unusual in some ways,
is enough like crude specimens from Kachemak Bay and Prince
William Sound (de Laguna, 1934, pl. 23, *1*; 1956, p. 25, *1*) and probably
Kodiak Island, to have come from any one of those places. The
same can be said for the well-made fragment, although the evidence
here more definitely suggests that this is a Kodiak lamp.

The collection also contains half of a *bullet mold* made from fine-
grained sandstone. This bullet mold section consists of one flat surface into which have been ground two circular depressions, each
roughly 1.5 cm. in diameter. At one end of either depression is a
groove which, when the identical other half of the mold was fitted to
this one, would allow the lead to be poured in. The opposite side of
the implement has not been finished but is distinguished by a distinct
lashing groove (pl. 2, *n*). The two halves of the mold would be lashed
tightly together before molten lead was poured, and then after the
metal had hardened, the halves could be separated and the completed
bullets removed.

## Wood

Artifacts of wood form by far the largest part of the Crow Village
collection, with 250 identifiable objects made from this material. Because of the large numbers and wide variety of types, the artifact descriptions have been grouped under 10 headings as follows: fishing,
land hunting, tools, household equipment, transportation, personal
adornment, tobacco complex, toys and games, ceremonial objects, and
miscellaneous and unidentified. It is hoped that by grouping the
wooden artifacts in this way, their significance in understanding the
pattern of living at Crow Village will be emphasized. It should be
noted at the outset that the types of wood employed for the manufacture of artifacts are spruce, birch, and cottonwood, with spruce
being used most frequently.

## FISHING

The number of artifacts connected with fishing is surprisingly small, considering the emphasis that one would expect to find on this form of subsistence in a river community. However, it should be remembered that artifacts of other materials will, when described, give a more complete picture of fishing as an activity.

As might be expected, objects associated with netting are of primary importance. Of the eight *mesh gages*, five are complete; four of these are for very small nets since the gaging distance on each is approximately 2.6 cm. (pl. 3, *k*, *p*). One of these specimens has a wrapping of spruce root around the distal end, perhaps for the purpose of enlarging the gaging distance (pl. 3, *p*). The other complete specimen has a gaging distance of 11.2 cm. (pl. 3, *o*), and two of the fragments are of approximately the same size. It seems likely that the smaller gages were used for seines or dip nets and the larger ones for gill nets.

Spruce *net floats*, of which there are four complete and three fragmentary specimens, are roughly rectangular in outline with laterally drilled holes at each end for attachment to the net. In cross section these implements have a rounded triangular form, narrow at the top, and thick at the bottom. The complete specimens range in length from 11.5 to 21.0 cm., and all are well made.

The single *net shuttle* recovered is very fragmentary, as both ends are badly broken. The main body of the shuttle is slightly concave on both sides and measures 11.5 cm. in length.

The one probable *fishing rod* is shuttle-shaped, 58 cm. in length, and slightly flattened on both sides. This rod is crudely made and is perhaps an unfinished specimen. A crudely made fragment with a single notched end also may be part of a fishing rod. It is likely that such implements were used for taking whitefish through holes in the ice.

## LAND HUNTING

Each of the three *blunt arrowheads* in the collection is distinctive. The first has a multifaceted tip which slopes to a long thin tang (pl. 3, *h*), while the second is broad and flat across the distal end and also slopes to a thin tang (pl. 3, *b*). The third is a spent rifle cartridge fitted over the end of a rounded shaft which slopes to a plain conical tang. The cartridge case is held in place with a crude metal rivet driven through both sides of the case and shaft (pl. 3, *c*).

There are eight spruce *bow* fragments in the collection, but only one is complete enough to provide information about the shape of the bow. This specimen, which is 78 cm. in length, is flat on one side and slightly convex on the other. The nock at the complete end has square shoulders and is rounded at the tip. Down the convex side of the specimen is a distinct groove which probably contained a sinew backing. Although this bow is not a toy, informants insisted that it was smaller than full size and probably would have been used by a boy. It is broken just below the constricted grip area. Five fragments, all approximately 14 cm. in length, are flat on both sides, and two of these have grooves for sinew of the type just described. The two other fragments have complete nock ends similar to the one already described (pl. 3, e).

Three shaft fragments of *bird spears* have grooves around the distal end into which barbed points would be set and lashed (pl. 3, m). The longest of these fragments is 43.5 cm., but the other two are much shorter. It should be pointed out that these implements could be associated with fishing just as well as with bird hunting.

Four small notched or grooved pieces of wood are identified as *snare parts* although they are not distinctive enough to make the identification certain. Three specimens are grooved at one end, presumably to hold a cord, while a fourth has a wedge-shaped notch cut in a similar position. One of the grooved specimens shows traces of red paint within the groove (pl. 3, a, f).

TOOLS

The 19 splitting *wedges* vary in length from 2 to 19.5 cm. and average 12 cm. All are of the same type, being blunt at one end and tapering to a wedge-shaped tip at the other (pl. 4, g). None, however, shows signs of very prolonged use. A single specimen is charred on one side and has been used as a fire drill board.

The collection contains four end-hafted *beaver tooth drawknife handles*, an implement that was doubtless of considerable importance in woodworking. All four have curved oblong grips, and the distal ends are slotted deeply for hafting a tooth blade. Two specimens also are provided with a lip to aid in lashing the tooth into the slot (pl. 4, f). The illustrated example has the proximal end formed into an animal's head with the eyes and mouth represented by slits cut into the wood.

There are three implements identified as *engraving tool handles*. The best of these is slotted at one end to receive a small animal tooth or iron blade and has a lip to aid in hafting. The main body of the handle has a series of attractively arranged raised bands in the characteristic fashion of Alaskan Eskimo engraving tool handles (pl. 4, d). The other two specimens are more crudely made; both have split ends and lashing grooves.

The two *ulu handles* are quite distinctive. One is curved to fit the shape of the blade and has a blade slit that runs the entire length of the specimen (pl. 4, e). The other is rectangular in shape with a

straight blade slit. This handle also has an oblong hole in the center
to aid in gripping the tool (pl. 4, *i*). The blade slits of both specimens
are narrow and probably would have been fitted with metal blades.

Two *scraper handles* for end-hafted stone scrapers indicate the
manner in which previously described blades were hafted. One
handle, which is straight with a rounded proximal end, has a flat
lashing bed with a lip on the opposite side to aid in hafting (pl. 4, *c*).
The second handle is short and oval with a flat projection at one end
to which a very small blade would be lashed (pl. 4, *j*).

One of the two cottonwood *adz handles* is approximately 71 cm. in
length and has a single large hole and lashing lip at the blade end
through which lashing was passed to attach the adz blade. The
other specimen, crudely made and approximately 43 cm. long, utilizes
the natural bend in a cottonwood branch. The outer surface of the
bent end is flattened for the attachment of a blade. Both of these
handles, because of their length, were probably for splitting adzes
that would have been hafted directly to the handles without the
use of a head of any kind.

Each of the four *fire drill shafts* is round in cross section; they
vary in length from 24 to 34 cm. and taper to a blunted point at the
distal end. All have been broken at the proximal end (pl. 4, *a*).
Another similarly shaped implement has a deep slot and lashing lip
at the distal end (pl. 4, *h*). This *drill shaft* would probably have held
a large stone or metal bit.

Another tentative identification is necessary with regard to three
so-called *strap drill handles*. Such handles would be attached to
loops of cord. Two handles would have a length of cord between
and a cord would be wrapped around a drill shaft. One handle is
cylindrical in shape with a groove around the middle for the cord
attachment. A second specimen is similar but more elaborately made
and has a wider groove with squared edges (pl. 3, *j*), while a third
is rectangular with a rectangular hole in the center (pl. 3, *i*).

Three cottonwood *mauls* were recovered, two of considerable size.
All three have large, heavy heads tapering to thin circular handles,
and show signs of considerable use. Both of the very large specimens
exceed 55 cm. in length and would probably have been used for driving
large stakes. The illustrated specimen has a much shorter handle
than the others (pl. 4, *b*). A fourth implement of spruce has been
identified as a maul largely on the basis of use. It is 32 cm. in length
and paddle shaped. One side of the broad, paddlelike surface is
deeply worn from pounding.

Six relatively light sharpened sticks are identified as *stakes* since
there seems to have been no other way in which they could have been
used. All are sharpened at one end, and the two complete specimens

show signs of having been pounded at the proximal end.  All are of
a size that would be suitable for use with canvas tents.

Four large, *flat cutting boards* were recovered, but none is complete.
All are comparatively thin pieces of wood, and one is approximately
60 cm. in length.  Two specimens show signs of having been worked
to a definite shape, probably rectangular, while the others are irregularly shaped pieces that simply were picked up to serve temporarily
as cutting boards.

A single *handle*, such as might have been used with a bucket, is
roughly semicircular in cross section and has end notches for hafting
(pl. 5, *h*).

There are five nearly complete *ladles*, all of which have straight
handles and broad bowls.  The variation shown is in bowl shape.
Two specimens have relatively deep rounded bowls (pl. 5, *f*), while
three have oblong shallow bowls (pl. 5, *d*).  Traces of red painted decoration are to be seen on two specimens.  A sixth fragment has a
long thin handle, but the shape of the bowl cannot be determined.
This example was apparently much thinner and lighter than the
others.

A wooden *poke stopper* with a deep lashing groove (pl. 5, *e*) is described here because it was probably a household item associated with
the storage of food or seal oil imported from the coast.  However, it
might also have been used as a float plug since it is likely that floats
were used by fishermen to mark the locations of their nets.

Although three fragmentary *vessel bottoms* were recovered, only one
is relatively complete.  This specimen, of which about half appears
to be present, was probably roughly square in shape with rounded
corners.  The bottom has a flat section near the center and flares
upward slightly a few centimeters from the sides.  The edges are
sharp, and the inside surface is flat except for an incised decoration
that appears to be a square with projections at the corners.  The
decorative lines are painted with red paint (pl. 5, *c*).  The other two
fragments identified as vessel bottoms have flat bases and sloping
sides similar to the one previously described.

*Vessel sides* vary in height from 1.8 cm., which is hardly more than
a rim, to 9.9 cm.  All five specimens are fragmentary, but with two it
is possible to determine the method of attachment to the vessel
bottom.  Both have narrow grooves running along the lower edge to
receive V-shaped projections on the vessel bottom.  Both also have
holes drilled through laterally at the level of the groove suggesting that
pegs helped to hold the bottom in place (pl. 5, *a*).  These vessel sides
were made of a single large flat piece of spruce which was bent to fit

the bottom and then fastened with root lashings as indicated in one illustration (pl. 5, *b*). The method of fastening the two very narrow specimens is not clear, but it is likely that they were grooved in a similar way and are the sides of relatively shallow oblong bowls.

Of the seven fragmentary *dishes*, four are complete enough to give a reasonable indication of the total size and shape. Two are oblong to round in shape and shallow with a relatively wide flat rim. The larger is approximately 25 by 21 cm., and the smaller, though incomplete, is almost as large. Two specimens are much longer than they are wide, have sides that slope up slightly, but have no distinct rim. Both of these are approximately 38 cm. in length and a little more than half as wide. One has been used extensively as a cutting board and is perhaps a meat dish. The other three fragments are from the flat bottoms of dishes and have no sides or rim.

A *shallow bowl* of spruce wood is fragmentary and has a flat bottom, steeply sloping sides and a flat rim. The bowl is deep and oblong in shape (pl. 5, *g*).

An interesting and unusual item of household equipment is a carefully shaped *bench plank support*, three of which were found beneath the bench planks in H–4. These objects look so much like stools that they would have been described as such had not two of them been found upright in place under the bench. All are made from spruce and measure approximately 18 cm. across the top and 21 cm. high. They have flat tops which are wider than the bottoms. Two specimens constrict around the middle and then flare out near the base. The third slopes gently to a base which is 8 cm. narrower than the top.

Three *lampstands* were recovered from H–1 and H–4 (see figs. 1, 4). H–4 contained a pair of these stands, one at each side of the dwelling in front of the back bench. One was made from a spruce burl and trunk, while the second was a small spruce trunk set upside down in the ground with a large basal root cut flat on top as the stand. The H–1 stand was made from a burl and trunk with the burl cut horizontally at the midpoint. Each is approximately 60 cm. high and about 25 cm. across the top. The burls are finished carefully to form a slightly concave platform for the lamp, and taper down to the natural shape of the log; the bases are about 12 cm. in diameter and were driven into the ground.

### TRANSPORTATION

Wooden artifacts functionally linked with travel are grouped into the following categories: kayak parts and boating equipment; sled and snowshoe parts. Kayak parts, although not numerous, are identified as of the same type which was used throughout southwestern Alaska in recent times and is still being used by some lower Kuskokwim River and adjacent coastal Eskimos. This type of kayak, with an inverted

V-shaped deck, a large mooring hole at the bow, and a projecting stern piece, is illustrated from Nunivak Island by Nelson (1899, pl. LXXIX, 2).

*Kayak frame parts* in the collection include a bow fragment which, although broken, shows part of the characteristic mooring hole. There is also a 35-cm. long section of the ring around the manhole. This section is 4.5 cm. wide, is grooved in the center on the outside, and has laterally drilled lashing holes to aid in fastening the skin cover tightly around the manhole. Also included is a single side support for the manhole ring (pl. 6, *m*). This specimen has a broadly concave base in order to fit into the side stringer, while the top surface is flat. There is a lashing hole on either side near the top for attachment to the ring, and a section of root lashing may be seen in one of the holes. A curved decorative line runs on the outer side near the top at the level of the lashing holes. Just above the narrow bottom are two lashing holes, with a lashing groove on the inner side for lashing to the stringer. A single deck support piece is semilunar in shape and probably would have fitted directly in front of or behind the manhole. No bottom or deck stringers were identified, but two ribs were found. These are approximately 15 cm. in length, wedge shaped at the top to fit into the side stringer, and notched at the bottom to receive the bottom stringer. Just above the notch in each specimen is a square lashing hole (pl. 6, *g*).

Seven sections of *single-bladed paddles* were recovered. Three of these are crutch handle pieces (pl. 6, *c*), and the other four are blade sections. One of the blades has a rounded tip, well worn from scraping (pl. 6, *f*), while three have a central ridge on both sides. The fourth blade section is almost complete. The ridge on this specimen terminates just at the point where the blade begins to broaden out; the blade itself is flat.

A single fragmentary *canoe* or *kayak sled crosspiece* is semicircular in cross section and has a lashing lip at the complete end to aid in lashing the crosspiece directly to the stanchions. The specimen is 21 cm. in length.

Sled parts are represented by a single stanchion, three runner sections and two shoes. The *sled stanchion*, or upright, is in very poor condition. Such an upright would extend from the runner to the crosspieces which hold the two runners together. On either side of this type of sled and above the crosspieces is a longitudinal wooden strip extending from the front to the back of the sled. Each crosspiece is lashed to this longitudinal strip by a thong that passes through the hole in the sled upright and over the strip. This hole and flat upper surface can be seen in the illustrated specimen (pl. 6, *l*). The lower end of the upright is wedge shaped to fit a slot in the runner.

Two of the sprucewood *sled runner sections* are short, averaging approximately 30 cm. in length and 5 cm. in height.  Each contains a single stanchion slot, rectangular in shape, 4.5 by 1.8 cm.  These slots extend about 1.8 cm. into the runner.  On one of these sections a nail has been driven into the stanchion hole, presumably to help hold the stanchion in place.  The third runner section is 81 cm. in length and, since it is from the front section of a sled, shows a decided upward curve at one end.  At the base of the curve the runner thickens and is 4.5 cm. in height.  At the beginning of the thickened section is a stanchion slot 5.0 by 1.5 cm. and extending 1.2 cm. into the runner.  Just below the slot a small hole has been drilled laterally through the runner, probably for lashing the end of the stanchion into the runner.

Of the two *sled shoe sections*, one is 54 cm. in length and 4.3 cm. wide, flat on the inside and rounded on the outer surface.  Two holes, approximately 8 mm. in diameter, have been drilled for pegging the shoe to the runner.  The other section is similar except that it is 146.5 cm. in length and must be nearly a complete shoe.  It is somewhat narrower (3.4 cm.) and much thicker (1.4 cm.) than the previously described section.  There are 10 irregularly spaced pegging holes, approximately 8 mm. in diameter, drilled through the shoe.  Some of the holes are close together, and in six the remains of wooden pegs can be seen.

The single cottonwood *snowshoe frame section*, although it does not reveal anything definite about the snowshoe style, at least suggests a type similar to that illustrated by Nelson (1899, fig. 64) from Cape Darby.  The recovered section seems to be a part of the frame near the front of the shoe.  There is a single slot, presumably to receive a crosspiece, and two laterally drilled holes for the webbing (pl. 6, *b*).

### PERSONAL ADORNMENT

Three lateral *labrets* and a single medial labret are the only wooden objects of personal adornment.  Two of the former are slightly oval in cross section and flare at the proximal end to form a retaining lip (pl. 6, *i*).  A third specimen is similar but larger and unfinished.  All have slightly concave inner surfaces.  The one artifact tentatively identified as a medial labret appears to be unfinished.  It is broad and rounded with a distinctly concave inner surface and two knoblike projections, one on each side, to form a retaining lip (pl. 6, *d*).  However, the identification of this specimen is uncertain.

### TOBACCO COMPLEX

Although there are no pipes represented in the collection, a number of artifacts can be associated with a tobacco complex.  Of particular interest is an oval *snuffbox*, described here because it has a wooden

top and bottom.   The sides of this well-made specimen are constructed
from a single piece of birchbark, the ends of which are notched and
interlocked.   A number of incised lines on both sides serve as decoration.   The wooden top and bottom pieces are neatly fitted, and at
the center of the lid is a small hole through which a cord would have
been placed as a handle (pl. 7, *g*).   This snuffbox resembles one from
St. Michael illustrated by Nelson (1899, pl. LXXXVI, *5*).

There are 13 artifacts identified as *tops or bottoms for snuff, tobacco,
or fungus boxes*.   The latter would contain the fungus ashes that
were mixed frequently with tobacco to extend its use (Nelson, 1899,
p. 271).   Eight specimens are round and range in size from 5.5 to
3 cm. in diameter.   Three have lips on one surface and small holes
in the center (pl. 7, *i*).   These are almost certainly lids, while the
others probably are bottoms.   All are slightly concave on one surface.
Oblong box lids or bottoms are represented by five specimens ranging
from 5.3 to 16.5 cm. in length.   Three of these are similar to the
former figure, and one has a hole in the center (pl. 7, *h*).   The two
large specimens may be bottoms for trinket boxes rather than parts
of smoking equipment.

GAMES AND TOYS

Four *tops*, two of which are complete, are slightly ovate in cross
section and thicken toward the center where there is a laterally drilled
hole.   A portion of a wooden spinning peg is still in the hole of one
specimen (pl. 8, *e*).   A game played with tops by Eskimo children
along the lower Yukon River is described by Nelson (1899, p. 333).

Two small, triangularly shaped flat-bottomed objects are identified
as *checkers* (pl. 7, *e*) since they closely resemble the wooden checkers
sometimes used today by Eskimos of the Bering Sea coast.

A surprisingly numerous group of 26 specimens are identified as
*flip darts*.   To play the game in which these pieces were used, a hole
would be made in the floor of the *kashgee* and the players would
attempt to flip "darts" into the hole (see Nelson, 1899, p. 332).
Each specimen is roughly the shape of an elongated diamond.   From a
sharp tip, the object swells at a point approximately one-third of the
distance from the distal end and from there tapers gently until it is
flat and wedge shaped at the proximal end.   There is considerable
variation in this general form.   Some of the gaming pieces are thick
and relatively heavy, while others are almost flat.   Some are short
and stubby at the proximal end, while others are thin and elongated.
Two specimens are illustrated to show the range of variation (pl. 7,
*a, b*).

Darts to be thrown at a target are represented by four specimens,
all of which thicken in the center and then taper back to a point at
the proximal end.   In the distal end of one specimen is inserted a

nail (pl. 7, *n*), and it is likely that the others were similarly tipped. Another specimen has two parallel lines circling it in the center as decoration. A dart game, as it was played at St. Michael in the late 19th century, is described by Nelson (1899, p. 333).

Two of the four *storyknives* are similar to those illustrated by Nelson (1899, pl. xcIV) and Oswalt (1952, pl. 6, *14*) in having plain straight handles which broaden out to form a semilunar blade (pl. 7, *l*). The other two, however, are quite different. While retaining the broad semilunar blade, the handles are curved and have two centrally placed projections. In the larger of the two (pl. 7, *j*) these projections could serve as a sort of grip, but this would not be possible in the case of the smaller lighter implement (pl. 7, *k*). Another characteristic of these specimens is that they resemble a short-legged animal with a long bushy tail. Storyknives are used by girls in the Kuskokwim River region to draw pictures in mud or snow to illustrate stories (Oswalt, 1952, p. 70; 1964).

The four *toy bow* fragments vary considerably in length. One fragment includes only a small section below the nock, while three others are considerably larger. One of these is 42 cm. in length and is virtually complete. All have nocks similar to the illustrated specimen (pl. 7, *o*).

A *toy salmon dart head*, the only example of such an implement in the entire collection, has two barbs on one side, a blade set in a blade slit at right angles to the barbs, and a broken base tapering to what was probably a conical tang (pl. 8, *k*). Both the single *toy dish* (pl. 7, *c*) and a *toy bucket bottom* are faithful reproductions of the full-sized object. A *toy boat* is so crude that the identification must be considered doubtful.

A group of four fragmentary, but roughly similar, implements have been identified as *toy leister prongs*. They are barbed on one side only and vary greatly in size. At one extreme is a very long specimen with three widely spaced barbs (pl. 3, *n*), while at the other extreme is a small specimen, also with three barbs (pl. 3, *d*). A single fragmentary *toy center prong* for a fish spear has two small barbs on one side and a shoulderless wedge-shaped tang (pl. 3, *l*). An unusual single-barbed fragment has a wide deep blade slot and may be the distal end of a *toy lance* (pl. 3, *g*).

The grip section of what appears to be a *toy pistol* is one of the more intriguing specimens in this category. The pistol seems to have been constructed to shoot something, and yet the method of its operation could not be established. Near the upper part of the grip is a square hole for a trigger, and immediately in front of this is a rectangular opening 4.5 cm. in length (pl. 7, *d*).

Almost as intriguing are four limb sections of what appears to have been a large segmented *doll*. Parts of both arms and legs are present, and they are flattened at the proximal ends for attachment to a torso. The one complete leg section is illustrated (pl. 7, *m*). The largest arm section, with the hand missing, is 36.5 cm. in length.

Seven animal carvings are all different and will have to be described individually. It should be pointed out that it is by no means certain that these carvings are toys. At least some of them may have been associated with ceremonies. The best examples are two sculptured carvings of a pregnant *bear* and a *mink* (pl. 8, *d*, *f*). The latter is in a poorer state of preservation. A *caribou* carving has no legs and exists in crude outline form only (pl. 8, *h*). Of the three flat outline carvings, two are grotesque, perhaps mythological creatures. One resembles a "*serpent*" (pl. 8, *j*), while the other, broken in the field but actually symmetrical, is an *ermine* with its back arched (pl. 8, *g*). The third flat carving obviously represents a bird, perhaps a *loon*, swimming (pl. 7, *f*). The final carving is a rough, unfinished *caribou head*.

### CEREMONIAL OBJECTS

The most abundant form of wooden ceremonial objects is the *memorial image*, of which there are eight examples. Five are carvings of caribou which, though different in size, are constructed similarly. The two largest specimens average 39 cm. in length and are approximately 12 cm. in height. The animal is represented in outline form, with the tail and eyes indicated but without antlers or legs. In the center of the underside of the animal is a rectangular slot to receive the stick on top of which the figure would rest. Two other animal carvings are somewhat smaller, averaging 28 cm. in length, but otherwise do not differ from those previously described except in having elongated necks and more clearly defined mouths (pl. 9, *a*). The fifth and smallest carving is the most carefully made. In addition to having an overall shape that is more cariboulike, this figure has inset eyes and also has been provided with drilled holes to receive antlers and four legs; parts of the wooden legs are still in place (pl. 8, *a*). Also considered as memorial images are one fragmentary and one complete human figure. The complete specimen, roughly made with the features barely indicated, has a small sliver of wood protruding from one side of the chest (pl. 9, *b*). The fragmentary carving is similar, but the head and stakelike base are missing   A questionable object in this category is what appears to be an animal head of some kind that terminates in a square peg for insertion into some larger object (pl. 8, *b*). It is too large for a mask appendage and too poorly preserved for exact identification.

Memorial images similar to those described above are illustrated from Cape Vancouver (Nelson, 1899, fig. 104). Nelson was told that they represented people who had been lost and whose bodies never had been recovered. He was informed further "that the grave-yards of the villages on the Kuskokwim, below Kolmakof Redoubt, are full of remarkable images of carved wood" (Nelson, 1899, p. 319). It is likely that the images described above were placed over graves and represented events in the life of the deceased or some aspect of his character and abilities. The wooden peg protruding from the chest of one carving may indicate the manner of death.

The three complete *masks* that were recovered are illustrated (pls. 15, 16), and no attempt will be made to describe them except to say that one (pl. 16, *b*), having no eyeholes, is either unfinished or was not intended to be worn. If the latter is true, this mask may have been fastened to a memorial board similar to the one from Big Lake (Nelson, 1899, fig. 105). There are four mask fragments, each of which is different. Two are too small to provide much information about the complete mask; the other two, however, will be described in some detail. The first is half of a mask that appears to have had a large aperture in the center since broken surfaces are to be seen only at the upper and lower ends. Two tufts of human hair, held in place with wooden pegs, are to be seen projecting from the outer edge of the specimen (pl. 9, *d*). The second mask segment may be considerably less fragmentary than it appears at first glance. It is a nose section, and although the specimen is in very poor condition, it is possible to see small depressions on either side of the nose which facilitated vision. Directly beneath the nose is a hole drilled at right angles to it; a cord might have passed through this hole and encircled the head. If this interpretation is correct, then the mask is virtually complete and was intended to be nothing more than a false nose (pl. 9, *c*).

The *mask appendages* are nearly all similar to those illustrated by Nelson. These include a boat model and two wands (pl. 8, *i, l*). Not illustrated by Nelson are two stylized animal or bird heads (pl. 8, *o*) that seem likely to have been associated with masks. More doubtful is a thin strip of wood, round in cross section, approximately 85 cm. in length and curved into a circle, which is tentatively identified as an encircling ring for a mask such as is illustrated by Nelson (1899, pl. CIII, *5*).

It is likely that the two *fish carvings* were used in ceremonies. One is a simple outline of a fish, while the second has the gills indicated and also has a suspension groove running entirely around it near the center. Remains of a root suspension cord can be seen in parts of the groove (pl. 8, *n*). These carvings are approximately the same size, and it may be that the plain one is unfinished.

The one *drum handle* is round in cross section toward the proximal end but flattens to a point inside the drum. There is a deep notch cut in one side for rim attachment (pl. 8, *m*).

A wooden *carving of a flower* is described here with the thought that it may have been used in connection with a ceremony, perhaps even in a service of the Russian Orthodox Church (pl. 8, *c*).

### MISCELLANEOUS AND UNIDENTIFIED

The use of wooden *pegs* for such diverse purposes as fastening human hair to the side of a mask and shoes to the bottom of a sled runner has been mentioned previously. Three unassociated pegs were recovered, two of which are approximately 3 cm. in length, 8 mm. in diameter, and tapered to a point at one end. The illustrated specimen is flat at both ends and 7 mm. in diameter (pl. 6, *h*). In addition, there are two unidentified fragments with pegs still in place. One of these is rectangular in shape and cut straight at one end suggesting part of a small box, the sides of which were pegged together.

As might be expected in a site where the wood preservation is as good as it is at Crow Village, there are large numbers of unidentifiable worked fragments. These objects, of which there are a total of 118, appear to have been broken either in the process of manufacture or in use. In many cases the objects could doubtless be identified were they not so fragmentary, but others probably would defy identification even if complete. In addition, there are 10 complete artifacts, the use of which is equally puzzling. No attempt will be made to describe all of them, but four are illustrated and deserve some special comment and speculation. Two objects that are spatulate shaped at one end may possibly be *bark peelers* (pl. 6, *a*). One of them is 80 cm. in length, which seems rather large for such an implement, and neither is curved sufficiently at the distal end. However, birchbark was of considerable importance to the people of Crow Village, and there are no other tools of any material that can be identified as bark peelers. A triangularly shaped object, pointed at one end, concave at the other, and semicircular in cross section, suggests to us a stylized bird in flight (pl. 6, *k*). It may be a mask appendage. A small stick, carefully worked and bluntly pointed at both ends, is charred at one end and has a crudely carved human face on one surface (pl. 6, *e*). A carefully worked object is an almost perfect egg shape and may have been a toy (pl. 6, *j*).

### BONE AND ANTLER

The number of recovered bone and antler artifacts is surprisingly small, and this fact, together with the relatively small number of unworked bones recovered, suggests that big game hunting was not an important subsistence activity.

Four *net sinkers* are made of antler and have a hole drilled laterally through each end. They are roughly similar in shape to previously described wooden net floats. A single bone sinker is oblong and notched at either end for attachment (pl. 10, *a*).

An interesting whalebone artifact, one of the few artifacts definitely associated with firearms, is a section of a *ramrod* (pl. 10, *q*). Presumably the rod would have been at least half again as long as it is now. At the distal end are four parallel raised ridges which encircle the specimen. Such an implement, which was made in imitation of a metal rod of European or American manufacture, could also be used for cleaning the weapon.

An open-socketed, antler, bladelike implement is identified as an *arrowhead*, although it could equally well be a knife blade. A long thin tang is flattened on one side to form a deep socket to receive the shaft (pl. 10, *e*). Above the tang the blade flattens out but is ridged on both sides.

The importance of woodworking is again emphasized by the occurrence of 11 antler *wedges*. They vary in length from 6.5 to 14 cm. and resemble previously described wooden specimens.

*Awls* are divided into two types. The first type is represented by two specimens made from split pieces of bone and worked to a fine point at one end (pl. 10, *h*). Type 2 awls, of which there are also two, are made from sections of antler tine, blunt at one end and sharpened to a point at the other end (pl. 10, *l*). A fifth specimen, tentatively identified as an awl, is made of bone. It is pointed at one end and spatulate shaped at the other (pl. 10, *i*). Such an artifact conceivably could have been used as a bark peeler.

A single antler *ulu handle* is roughly rectangular in shape but slightly concave along the side that is gouged out to receive the blade. This is one of the few decorated specimens in the collection. On each side a set of lines parallel the base of the implement, with a series of evenly spaced drilled dots between them. At both ends, as well as in the center, are parallel lines extending vertically around the handle to the horizontal lines on the opposite side (pl. 10, *k*).

An antler *side bladed knife handle*, the familiar Eskimo "crooked knife," has a slightly curved blade slit and lashing lip at one end, and a deep groove with rivet holes at the other. This slot may have been for a blade or chisel, but is more likely for an extension of the handle (pl. 10, *f*).

A large roughly worked basal section of an antler tine has a hole gouged out of one end and is flattened on one side. It is possible that this implement is an unfinished close-socketed *adz head*.

There are 12 sections of whalebone *sled shoes* ranging in length
from 4.5 to 36.5 cm. Several have sawed surfaces, and all have
holes for attachment to the runner. They resemble the previously
described wooden sled shoes. On one shoe section a partly drilled
peg hole indicates that a metal woodworking bit, probably fitted to
a brace, was used for the drilling.

A single antler *kayak shoe* fragment was recovered. Such shoes
were attached to the stem and stern of a kayak so that the cover
would not tear as the vessel was drawn up on the beach (pl. 10, *g*).

A bear tooth has a drilled hole at the proximal end, indicating its
use as a *pendant* or as part of a necklace (pl. 10, *m*).

Four worked antler fragments show signs of having been cut with a
metal saw.

## CLAY

A small number of pottery fragments, both from lamps and cooking
pots, constitute the entire assemblage of clay artifacts from the site.
The cooking pots will be described first, and in this connection it
should be mentioned that in the case of smaller sherds, there was
some difficulty in separating lamp and pot fragments.

Among the 61 *potsherds* recovered are 8 rim sherds, 7 of which show
surface treatment of the Yukon Line-Dot type (Oswalt, 1955, p. 37).
Five have two encircling horizontal lines just below the rim with
one row of dots immediately below the lines (pl. 10, *d*). A single
sherd has a row of dots alone. Four of these sherds have a series of
horizontal ridges on the inner surface, a form of surface treatment
that also is characteristic of four body sherds (pl. 10, *c*). One rim
fragment has a single interior ridge running horizontal to and just
below the rim. These Yukon Line-Dot decorated sherds all have
slightly flaring rims, but lip treatment varies to some extent. In
cross section the lip sherds are flat (one), flat and outward sloping
(one), flat with an incised groove around the top (three), and grooved
and outward sloping (two). The eighth rim fragment is from a plain
vessel with an inverted rim and flat inward sloping lip. An unusual
feature of one of the Yukon Line-Dot treated rim sherds is crudely
incised crossed lines just below the row of dots (pl. 10, *b*). In addition
to these rim sherds showing surface treatment, two sizable body sherds
show a pair of horizontal lines which apparently encircled the vessels
well below the rim. This also is a feature of the Yukon Line-Dot
type (Oswalt, 1955, p. 37).

On the basis of the potsherds recovered, nothing definite can be
said about the shape of the cooking vessels. However, the Yukon
Line-Dot form of surface treatment is generally associated with the
situla shape (Oswalt, 1955, p. 37), and the occurrence of two small

flat-bottomed sherds tends to confirm this as far as the Crow Village pottery is concerned.

All sherds were examined to determine the type of temper used in their manufacture. The temper proved to be predominantly inorganic, with only two sherds containing a combination of organic and inorganic tempering. The inorganic temper consists of sand, gravel, or small pebbles with the coarser material being the most common; grass is the only organic tempering material. The texture of the pottery is not particularly fine, but the tempering material seems to be distributed fairly evenly throughout the ware. Inorganic tempering protrudes through the surface in the majority of sherds.

To determine the thickness of the ware, all of the unexfoliated sherds were measured. The thickest was 12 mm., the thinnest 4 mm., and the average about 7 mm. Nearly all the potsherds from cooking vessels are gray-black or black in color, but the range is black to buff with a few sherds of an extremely light brown.

The 15 *lamp sherds* are fragments of shallow, saucer-shaped containers and all are tempered with either gravel or pebbles. Ten sherds show a series of grooves running around the bowl (pl. 10, *j*). The most grooves visible on any one sherd is seven, and on one of these sherds the grooves appear to reach almost to the center of the lamp. Seven sherds of this type include a section of the rim, and on all but one specimen there is some kind of decorative treatment of the rim. One sherd has three encircling lines outside the rim, two have two such lines, and two have a single line. A single sherd has a deep, encircling groove rather than a simple incised line. It is possible that lamps with this style of surface treatment would have a cross at the center of the bowl (Oswalt, 1953, p. 18, pl. *1, 6, 8, 9*) or they may have had undecorated centers (Oswalt, 1953, pl. *1, 7*). A single fragment which represents almost half of a medium sized vessel has a deep bowl and five encircling lines near the rim. The center of this lamp was apparently undecorated (pl. 10, *n*). It may be that some of the lined sherds previously described come from a lamp of this type. Two sherds, including one rim fragment, are from undecorated lamps. The rim fragment is apparently from a very small vessel, and the rim itself turns up only slightly, while the lip is flat.

The largest lamp sherd in the collection has a large shallow bowl and a sharply turned up rim. The lip is flat with an incised groove running around the top. On the inside of the bowl is a pair of encircling lines well below the rim, followed by a set of three similar lines near the center of the vessel (pl. 10, *o*). The final lamp fragment represents almost half of a very small vessel, perhaps a hunter's lamp or a toy. There are four encircling lines running around the lamp below the rim and a triple-lined central cross (pl. 10, *p*).

## GRASS

Artifacts of grass are not numerous in the collection, but they do reveal some uses of this material. At several places in the excavated portion of the midden, bunches of grass were found. These may represent grass collected for plaiting into rope or for other uses. It is worth noting that grass was woven into socks and used for insoles in the Yukon-Kuskokwim region (Nelson, 1899, p. 43).

A large number of *plaited grass rope* fragments were recovered, of which the illustrated specimen is typical (pl. 11, *f*). A two-strand twisted section of *grass netting* consists of meshes about 5 cm. square (pl. 11, *i*). A number of small sections of *woven grass* were recovered from H–3 and H–4 (pl. 11, *g*). These might be part of grass bags or grass matting, both of which were used extensively in the Yukon-Kuskokwim region (Nelson, 1899, pp. 202–205).

## BARK AND ROOT

Among the most significant facts impressed upon the excavators as they worked in the site was the importance of birchbark to the former occupants. Hardly a shovelful of dirt could be moved without encountering strips of bark, and on more than one occasion the presence of large numbers of cut bark sections hindered excavation to a marked degree. The importance of this material in house construction has already been mentioned, and it now remains to describe birchbark artifacts.

It is doubtless true that much of the birchbark collected was made into *baskets*. Nine complete or nearly complete baskets were recovered along with fragments of many more. A few bark baskets were remarkably well preserved, but the majority crumbled into fragments as soon as they dried. Thus the number of baskets might have been much larger, and the general tendency for all birchbark fragments to crumble makes it difficult to arrive at an accurate count of the number of recovered specimens. The complete baskets are all of the same type. That is, they are all made from a single piece of bark folded at two ends to form a basket and then stitched, usually with spruce root. Even the complete baskets are badly twisted and crushed, and therefore it is difficult to obtain accurate measurements. Perhaps it is sufficient to say that there is a great variation in size. The recovered fragment appears to represent about half a basket which must have, when complete, measured at least 18 cm. long and 30 cm. wide. At the other extreme, a complete specimen appears to have been about 7 cm. square.

Of the 18 fragments of worked birchbark, at least 7 are definitely parts of baskets. The method of sewing is more clearly seen on the fragments than in the complete baskets.   As mentioned previously, it would seem that most baskets were sewn with spruce root as shown in the illustrated specimen (pl. 11, *b*).   For this type of sewing, widely spaced and fairly sizable holes are required.   However, at least three fragments have very closely spaced and small sewing holes suggesting that a finer material, perhaps finely braided grass, was used (pl. 11, *c*). Many of the unidentified sewn birchbark fragments probably are parts of baskets, but this cannot be determined with any degree of certainty.   All of these fragments have widely spaced holes for spruce root stitching, and a number of them have fragments of root still in place (pl. 11, *e*).   On six fragments, but on none of the complete baskets, are markings in red paint.   In every case this consists of a band of red next to the row of stitching holes (pl. 11, *a*).   It should also be noted that birchbark was used in the manufacture of a snuffbox described previously.

Before leaving the subject of birchbark baskets, it might be well to mention that they were used for cooking and were undoubtedly the most important cooking vessels even though metal cooking ware was known to the Eskimos and occurs in the collection.   In all the houses there were fire cracked beach pebbles of the kind that would have been used for stone boiling, and in H–3 a cluster of these stones was found near the fireplace.

The only other bark artifacts in the collections are *net floats* made of cottonwood bark.   The 11 complete specimens range in length from 12 to 26 cm., although nearly all are closest to the former figure. In construction they resemble the previously described wooden net floats.   In addition to the complete floats, there are 19 fragments and 5 sections of bark that are probably net float blanks.

The importance of spruce root for stitching baskets, lashing kayak frames, and other uses, already has been stressed.   In the collection are several additional examples of the use of spruce root that should be mentioned.   There are three fragments which show two pieces of wood bound together with root lashing (pl. 11, *d*), and the handle fragment of an unidentified wooden object is wrapped with spruce root, presumably to provide a better grip (pl. 11, *j*).   From H–3 was recovered a bundle of root in prepared form that would be constantly on hand for use in a variety of household tasks (pl. 11, *h*).

## METAL

The artifacts described thus far in this chapter are of indigenous manufacture.   That is, presumably they were made by Eskimos at the site.   Identifying such artifacts has given little difficulty since the materials are associated with traditional Eskimo material culture. However, when it comes to a description of metal artifacts, the problem of identifying indigenous objects is not so simple. Some items made of metal are readily recognized as complete artifacts brought to the site and used intact by the Eskimos. Others are just as readily identifiable as attempts by the Eskimos to work in a new medium and adapt old forms to a new material. But in between these two extremes are a number of artifacts that could belong to either category. Some are crudely made and suggest local manufacture, while others are so poorly preserved that it is difficult to establish their provenience one way or the other. Therefore, the listing of some artifacts as of local manufacture should be considered as tentative.

By far the largest number of indigenously manufactured metal artifacts are made from tinned steel plate of the type normally used in the manufacture of tin cans. Used cans definitely provided the greatest amount of raw material for secondary reworking into artifacts. Although cast iron and other heavy metals apparently were available in small quantities, the Eskimos relied on can metal even when it was not particularly satisfactory for the purpose intended. Thus many of the metal artifacts seem nonfunctional, and one can imagine the disgust with which, for example, an Eskimo woman first used an ulu with a blade made of flimsy can metal. However, can and other metal could be cut and reworked more easily and rapidly than stone or other indigenous materials. It is not surprising that it was eventually favored for a variety of tools and household objects.

A single *salmon dart head* has been fashioned from a piece of iron, possibly a stove or cast iron kettle fragment. It has a pair of opposite barbs, a narrowed area near the base for attachment of the line, and a single spur (pl. 12, *a*).

Six lead *musket balls* of the type that would have been made in the stone bullet mold previously described were found in H–3. The balls have a burr running medially around them indicating the division of the two halves of the mold. These balls would have been used in a muzzle loading weapon with a barrel diameter of approximately 1.5 cm.

A light piece of metal, probably a can fragment, has been folded double for added strength and then turned up at one end to form a hook. Such an implement might have been used as a *pothook* (pl. 12, *d*).

*End bladed knife blades* of metal are much less common than might be expected, but there is a single crude blade that might have served such a purpose. It is heavily corroded, and thus its identification as an indigenously manufactured item is questionable. There is a short tang for insertion into the handle (pl. 12, *e*).

Two *saw blade* fragments appear to be narrow strips from can metal that has been notched by hand (pl. 12, *h*). Such a saw blade presumably would have been hafted into a wooden handle and could have been used for only very light work.

A badly corroded implement with a long, slender tip and a broad, flattened and notched base may have been hafted as an *awl* (pl. 12, *f*).

There are five *ulu blades*, all of which have been cut from the sides of cans. They vary in length from 10 cm. to 16.5 cm., and all are flat across the top and have a semilunar cutting edge (pl. 12, *n*).

Two *skin scraper blades* have been cut from the sides of cans and have slightly convex working edges. One specimen is of particular interest because it has been strengthened by having the edges folded on two sides (pl. 12, *b*). The second is shorter, 6.8 cm. in length, and tapers toward the proximal end.

Among the most interesting of the indigenously constructed metal artifacts are crude *dishes* or small containers, of which there are nine complete or nearly complete examples. They all are made from pieces of can siding that has been folded at the corners to form a container (pl. 12, *c*). All are extremely shallow, and most are roughly rectangular in shape, varying from 5.2 to 20.0 cm. in length. It is likely that the larger specimens were used in connection with food and eating. The smallest example, however, is folded at one end only and may have been a *scoop* or had some similar use (pl. 12, *i*).

A number of cut can fragments were most certainly used as *reinforcement pieces* since they have nail holes all around their sides (pl. 12, *j*). Four fragments are identified as having been used in this manner, and it is possible that other fragments of metal were intended for a similar use. Such reinforcement pieces might be used to strengthen the cracked shaft of a lance or to repair wooden artifacts in a variety of ways. Another type of reinforcement piece, the use of which is more difficult to determine, is a strip of metal approximately 5 cm. in width and 32 cm. long bent in a compressed S-shaped form at either end. These strips, of which four were found in H–4, are rounded as though to fit around a log used in house construction. In fact, these strips were found in association with the bench logs of H–4 but in such a way that it was not possible to determine their exact function. Nevertheless, it seems likely that they were used either to reinforce house construction logs or to aid in fastening bench planks to floor logs.

Of particular interest are the 26 *cut can fragments* which form the raw material out of which metal artifacts probably would have been manufactured. These show cutting in a variety of lengths and shapes, but one specimen is more revealing than the others. This is a roll of can metal and consists of three cans 8.4 cm. in height rolled together. The bottoms and tops of these cans have been cut out and the sides rolled up and stored for later use in the manufacture of artifacts.

In addition to the cut can fragments, two sections of bucket handles have been cut for future use, and a single piece of cut sheet copper was found.

A small copper *ferrule* apparently was made to fit over the end of of a small shaft or stick. It is decorated with a series of engraved parallel lines horizontally encircling the specimen and another series of short parallel lines engraved at right angles to them (pl. 12, *k*).

Four .22-caliber rifle cartridges have been drilled at the proximal end for stringing as *beads* to form a bracelet or necklace. Fragments of the twisted grass on which these cartridges were strung still are visible in the drilled holes. All of the cartridges were found in the same house and presumably were strung together. Another cartridge of undetermined caliber is similarly drilled, has grass stringing material knotted on the inside, and two beads still attached to the outside.

## Glass

Four pieces of heavy bottle glass have been extensively retouched for use as *scrapers*. Three are made from fragments of light-green glass ranging from 4 to 6 mm. in thickness, while a fourth is a fragment of dark-brown glass of similar thickness (pl. 12, *g*). In addition, two small scrapers are retouched fragments of window glass.

## Non-Eskimo Pottery

A single sherd of ironstone china with a purple transfer-printed floral design on one surface has been worked into a round shape for use as a *labret* (pl. 12, *m*). It has been grooved in such a way that each surface forms a lip to hold the labret in place.

## Leather

All three fragments of leather in the collection have been derived from commercially prepared cowhide. The largest is 15 cm. in length, while the other two are about half that size. They are described here because all three have been prepared as *patches* or *reinforcing sections*. They are carefully cut, and rows of stitching holes surround the outer edges (pl. 12, *l*).

## IMPORTED MANUFACTURED GOODS

Artifacts described under this heading are what normally are referred to as trade goods. That is, they were made elsewhere by non-Eskimos and traded to the residents of Crow Village, probably in exchange for furs or labor.

## Non-Eskimo Pottery

The excavations at Crow Village resulted in the recovery of 324 sherds of non-Eskimo pottery including 2 partially restorable vessels, a cup and a saucer. All the collected sherds are fragments of ironstone china, a stoneware varient that was extremely popular during the 19th century. In spite of the uniformity of the ware, there is considerable variation in the structure of the sherds themselves. In addition to variable thickness, it has been noted that some sherds are from vessels that were better fired than others, that some have a smoother glaze, and that exposure to the elements has resulted in differential surface deterioration.

Stone china, a type of stoneware, was first introduced by Spode and became popular because it was cheaper and more durable than porcelain. Its introduction was followed in 1813 by the "Patent Ironstone China" developed and patented by C. J. Mason and Company of Lane Delph, England, in that year. When Mason's patent expired, a number of other English potters began to make the ware (Blacker, n.d., p. 41; Fontana and Greenleaf, 1962, p. 92; Ormsbee, 1959, p. 3; Savage, 1959, p. 206). The body of ironstone is a mixture consisting of China clay, china stone, flint, and bone ash, glazed with borax flint and spar. The ware is fired to the point of vitrification and is extremely hard (Bemrose, 1952, p. 16; Savage, 1959, p. 19). Blacker (n.d., pp. 194–197) and others have noted that the utilitarian durability of ironstone ware and its relative inexpensiveness made it ideal for export in huge quantities. The same author estimates that at the time of writing (in the 1920's) fully one-third of the ironstone ware made in England was exported. This included not only tableware but also insulators and toilet fixtures. American potters apparently began to make ironstone ware in the 1870's (Barber, 1893, p. 200; Fontana and Greenleaf, 1962, p. 93).

The remarkable qualities of ironstone resulted in its being used extensively by the United States Army which carried it throughout the American west as the various military posts were established (Fontana and Greenleaf, 1962, p. 92). Since these same qualities would recommend the ware to distributors and traders providing goods of European and American manufacture to trading posts in Alaska, it is not surprising to find ironstone china in the Crow Village site.

The collection of non-Eskimo pottery can be classified most satisfactorily according to the three types of surface treatment: undecorated white ware, transfer-printed ware, and hand-decorated ware. The most common ware represented is undecorated and white. There are 164 sherds of this utilitarian pottery in the collection along with 1 nearly complete cup. Only rim and base sherds were saved; 98 body sherds were counted, noted as to house location, and then discarded. This ware is remarkably uniform although there is some variation in thickness, firing, and smoothness of the glaze. A single sherd has a drilled hole near one edge, indicating an attempt to repair a broken vessel by a method commonly used with traditional Eskimo pottery.

Transfer-printed ware is represented by 53 sherds and 1 nearly complete saucer. Transfer printing is an English development which spread during the 19th century. The method, said to have been invented by the Irish engraver, John Brooks, about 1753, is relatively simple. An engraved copper plate is inked with ceramic colors, a print is taken from it while the ink is still wet, and the paper pressed onto the ware. The piece of pottery is then immersed in water to float off the paper and fired to fix the color (Savage, 1959, pp. 29–30). The most common transfer print is the willow pattern, 15 sherds of which occur in the Crow Village collection (pl. 13, *a*). This design was first engraved by Thomas Minton for Thomas Turner of Caughley about 1780. This representation of a Chinese scene is a European invention derived from a number of Chinese sources (Savage, 1959, p. 31).

The transfer-printed ware from Crow Village tends to be somewhat thinner than the undecorated ware and has a smoother glaze. In addition to the willow pattern, other designs, mostly floral, are represented in brown, green, purple, black, and pink colors. Some of these floral representations are combined with geometric designs, and many have a distinctive oriental appearance.

The hand painted ware, of which there are 98 sherds, is approximately the same thickness as the plain ware and definitely thicker than the transfer-printed sherds. All designs appear to be floral and are crudely applied (pl. 13, *b*). Various shades of blue, green, red, and purple predominate. Painted lines around the inner and outer surfaces of the vessels, usually near the rim or base, are common.

In addition to the wares described above, there are three fragments of heavy ironstone with a thick brown glaze that are probably fragments of a teapot. Also there are three fragments of kitchen bowls decorated with thick light-blue lines.

As far as identifiable forms are concerned in plain ware, large heavy cups with slightly flaring sides constricting to a narrower flat bottom and with or without handles are common. Fragments of all types of ware appear to be from cups or saucers with the exception of two bowl sherds. There are no identifiable plate fragments. A number of flat bottom sherds suggest large heavy mugs with straight sides and indented bottoms. Some of these may have had faceted sides. Saucer fragments tend to be from deep vessels with smooth or scalloped rims. Generally speaking, all the ware, with the possible exception of a few transfer-printed saucer fragments, gives the impression of being heavy, crudely decorated, and highly utilitarian.

Unfortunately, the non-Eskimo pottery from Crow Village is not useful for dating within narrow limits. Ironstone ware is, of course, still being made, and design elements were so widely borrowed, both in the United States and England, that this element has no chronological significance. For example, willow pattern ware has been made in Staffordshire potteries since the late 18th century and is still being made. Also, several American potteries have been engaged in its manufacture for the past 60 years or more. Specimens of this ware from the Taral site on the Copper River were examined by C. Malcolm Watkins of the U.S. National Museum who felt that they had definite late 19th- or early 20th-century characteristics such as shade of color, sharply cut design, rounded saucer foot rims, and extreme hard whiteness (VanStone, 1955, p. 123). All of these characteristics are also present in the Crow Village willow pattern specimens.

Hand-painted ware similar to the Crow Village sherds also is still being made, and Watkins has noted, again with reference to similar material from the Taral site, that the more recent the ware, the more crude the application of color and design (VanStone, 1955, p. 123). The hand-painted ware from Crow Village is crude enough and certainly can date no earlier than the latter part of the 19th century.

Two bottom sherds have clearly visible hallmarks on them, but it has been possible definitely to identify only one of them. This mark consists of a circle within which is an American eagle with wings spread. Around the circle on the outside are the words "Semi-vitreous porcelain" and below this the notation "K.T. & K. Co." This is one of many hallmarks used by the firm of Knowles, Taylor & Knowles of East Liverpool, Ohio. The founder of this company, Isaac W. Knowles, was a salesman for James Bennett, the original East Liverpool potter, and set up his own pottery in 1845. After reorganization, the firm was known in 1870 as "Knowles, Taylor & Knowles," and began manufacturing ironstone china in 1873 (Cox, 1946, vol. 2, p. 1007; Thorn, 1947, p. 133). The second mark is fragmentary, and this has prevented a precise identification. Part of a lion and unicorn coat of arms is visible with the words "ironstone china" above. Comparison of this fragmentary mark with a variety of marks in Thorn, particular attention being paid to the positioning of the letters, seems to suggest that this may be one of the many marks used by the Steubenville Pottery Company of Steubenville, Ohio, a firm that was founded in 1879 (Thorn, 1947, p. 149). Whether or not this is a correct identification, the mark definitely resembles those of a number of large 19th-century Ohio potteries.

On the basis of hallmark identifications, then, it would seem that the ironstone ware from the site is mostly, if not entirely, of American manufacture. In 1891 the United States began to require that all imports, including pottery, be labeled with the name of the country of origin. Therefore, after 1891 all English pottery exported to the United States was marked "England" just as it is at the present time. In the Crow Village collection there are, in addition to the 2 pieces with hallmarks already described, 16 basal sherds large enough so that parts of hallmarks would be visible if they were present. Thus it is difficult to escape the conclusion that the majority of pottery used by the villagers was unmarked. Unmarked pottery must have been made in America, imported before 1891, or brought into the country through other than the usual import channels (Fontana and Greenleaf, 1962, p. 93; Ormsbee, 1959, pp. 16–17). Although it is impossible to say with any degree of certainty, there seems little reason to doubt that the Crow Village pottery is American and dates from the last three decades of the 19th century.

## GLASS

With the exception of beads, objects of glass and even glass fragments are not common in the Crow Village collection. If bottles, drinking glasses, and other glass artifacts had been used extensively, we would expect that they would have occurred in abundance since the material, though breakable, is impervious to decay. It therefore seems likely that glass, at least as a container material, was an unimportant aspect of the material culture.

### BUTTONS

Five milk glass buttons, all of the common four-hole shirt button variety, occur in the collection. They are molded in a biconvex shape with a slight depression in one face. All have large holes, and four are size 14 (mm.) while one is size 24 (mm.). Such buttons were first made in France and introduced to the United States about 1860 (Fontana and Greenleaf, 1962, p. 98).

### WINDOW GLASS

Fifty-nine fragments of window glass, forty-eight of which were discarded in the field, also are included in the collection. Most of the fragments are less than 2 mm. in thickness, although one piece is 5 mm. thick. A number of fragments have edges that are straight and smooth, suggesting the use of a glasscutter. It seems likely, therefore, that the Eskimos obtained the glass in the sizes required, the cutting being done at the store just as it is today. The most likely use for window glass would be as a covering for the skylight, replacing the traditionally used gut or fishskin covering. Two fragments of window glass have been retouched as scrapers and were described earlier.

BOTTLES

Four complete or nearly complete bottles were recovered, along with thirteen bottle fragments, three of which have been retouched as scrapers (previously described). The fragments include five pieces of thick dark-brown glass, one of which is a large basal fragment, while the others are either clear or of various shades of amber and green.

As far as bottle types are concerned, two complete specimens and two fragments are recognizable as being associated with patent medicines. All were presumably the same shape, being tall with rectangular bodies and "panels" on which the trade name might appear. One complete bottle of this type has no trade name (pl. 13, c), while the other has "California Fig Syrup Co., San Francisco, Cal." on the front panel, and "Syrup of Figs" on both sides. One panel fragment has an " 's" visible as well as the letters "pound" as part of the last word. This of course suggests that the contents were somebody's compound. The third complete bottle is of the shape one normally associates with soft drinks, but it contained an oily substance that smelled like a medicine (pl. 13, e). The fourth bottle (pl. 13, d) is of bluish glass and looks older than the others. It is rounded with a narrow neck and wide rim, but its use is unknown.

According to Hunt (1959, pp. 9–10), an easily recognized change in bottle styles took place about the time of World War I when the necks of bottles began to be finished by machine rather than by hand. "In the modern machine-finished bottle, the seams from the mold extend the whole length of two sides and even across the lip of the neck. Prior to World War I the necks were finished by hand, and the seams on bottles made during earlier periods end at the base of the neck which is a layer of glass wound around the partly finished bottle" (ibid., p. 9). This change to machine methods of bottle manufacture can be traced to the invention by M. J. Owens in 1898 of the first successful completely automatic bottle machine (Singer et al., 1958, vol. 5, pp. 675–676). Hunt further notes an earlier change in bottle style which took place about 1900 when metal caps were introduced. During the 1890's and earlier, most bottles had been made to receive cork stoppers (Hunt, 1959, p. 10). The importance of this information as far as the Crow Village bottles is concerned is that all four complete bottles have hand-finished necks and therefore certainly date before 1917. In addition, all four

bottles have necks made to receive cork stoppers, and in the case of
two specimens, the corks were still in place at the time of discovery.
This fact alone would tend to place the bottles chronologically where
we would expect to find them—at the end of the 19th century.

One other feature of manufacture and style is likely to be of value
when more research has been done on late 19th-century and early
20th-century glass bottles. This concerns the fact that molded
marks frequently occur on the bottoms of bottles and may indicate
the manufacturer, the contents, or both (Fontana and Greenleaf,
1962, p. 101). All four complete bottles from Crow Village and two
bottom fragments have molded marks. In three cases at least, these
marks indicate the name of the manufacturer but only one could be
identified definitely. This is "A & DH CO." which stands for the
Alexander and David H. Chambers Co. of Pittsburgh (Fontana and
Greenleaf, 1962, p. 101). Fontana and Greenleaf point out that
Arthur Woodward was able to delineate many of the marks found on
bottles at Fort Union, N. Mex., but was able to identify with certainty only three, including the one given above. It is clear, as these
authors take care to mention, that much more research needs to be
done on the entire subject of late 19th- and 20th-century bottles
(1962, p. 101).

### MISCELLANEOUS GLASS

In addition to buttons, window glass, and bottles, there are three
fragments of what appear to have been faceted *drinking glasses*.
Also there are two rather thin curved pieces that may be fragments of
*oil lamp chimneys*. If this identification is correct, it would be the
only indication in the Crow Village collection of the use of any kind
of lamp other than the traditional Eskimo clay variety.

### BEADS

Various types of glass trade beads were found in all houses and in
the two large midden sections. They form an important group of
artifacts whose structure, color, form, and size lend themselves to
typological analysis. Their value as dating aids, however, is limited,
and it will be possible to make only the most general statements concerning the chronological position of the Crow Village beads.

In general, the bulk of the glass beads traded on the North American
continent from the 16th until the first half of the 19th century were
made in the glass factories of Venice in Italy. After that time many
beads were manufactured in France and some in Czechoslovakia,
known then as Bohemia. A number of other countries imported
beads from Italy and repackaged them for shipment abroad (Woodward, 1959, n.p.; 1960, n.p.). The Crow Village beads, which are

undoubtedly of European manufacture, probably were made by one of two related processes. The single color beads were made by breaking a glass tube, composed of a single type of glass, into segments which then were tumbled in a heated drum to wear off the sharp edges. The white-lined and dark-green-lined beads were manufactured by fashioning two layers of different colored glass into a tube, breaking the tube into bead lengths, and again tumbling them in a heated drum. The latter beads have a central core of one color of glass and an outer coating of another (Duffield and Jelks, 1961, pp. 40–41; Orchard, 1929, pp. 82–83; Woodward, 1959, n.p.; 1960, n.p.).

Four hundred and sixteen beads of the various types make up the collection. For study purposes these were first separated into groups based upon color alone. The colors are given as they appear to us and not through comparison with a standard color chart. Gradations in color are often imperceptible, and many of the beads described also appear to be discolored because of changes caused by chemical actions of the soil or by firing. It was found that there were 250 white, 117 blue, 8 white-lined red, 3 green, 7 dark-green-lined red, 2 yellow, 7 red, 2 blue-lined white with alternate painted stripes, and 20 black. Next the beads were separated according to shape within each color group, and it was found that eight different types are represented (fig. 6). Sizing came next, and out of the total there were 16 of the "seed" form, those that do not exceed 2 mm. in diameter. However, there were a large number of beads averaging 3 to 5 mm. in diameter. All of the seed beads belong to type A and are invariably very brightly colored. Blue, white, black, and yellow are the colors represented, and these beads are generally similar to those sold in tubes in stores today for sewing into beadwork designs.

FIGURE 6.—Quarter sections of beads.

Of the 250 white beads, 163 belong to type B, 78 to type A, 8 to type E, and 1 to type D. The color varies from an extremely bright, hard whiteness that characterizes the five seed beads to a grayish white that is perhaps more typical of this category as a whole. The largest white beads belong to type E and average approximately 8 mm. in length. Of particular interest is the single milk-white bead belonging to type D. It was apparently cut from a hexagonal cane and is 1.5 cm. in length and 3 mm. in diameter.

The blue beads show the greatest variety of shapes and can be grouped into the following types: 55, type A; 29, type B; 18, type E; 8, type G; 6, type C; and 1, type F. There are nine seed beads, but a

great many more are just a little larger than the seed bead as defined
above. The color ranges from an extremely deep marine blue to the
very light blue that characterizes the beads of the seed form. The
largest blue beads, some measuring as much as 7 mm. in diameter,
belong to type B with the exception of the single type F specimen.
Of greatest interest, however, are the eight faceted beads, all a deep
marine blue, and all averaging approximately 6 mm. in length with
corresponding diameters. These beads were cut from a hexagonal cane,
and the facets appear to have been made by rubbing each bead against
some abrasive object to create a number of irregular facets over the
entire surface (Woodward, 1959, n.p.; 1960, n.p.).

The eight white-lined red beads all belong to type A and uniformly
have dark, translucent, orange-red exteriors and opaque white interiors.
This is a variety of the famous "Cornaline d'Aleppo" bead, the significance of which will be discussed later.

Three green beads, all belonging to type A, are of a uniform dark
green color. One is quite large, measuring 7 mm. in diameter, and is
more round than the others.

Of the seven dark-green-lined red beads, three belong to type A
and four to type B. All have an opaque, dull, reddish brown exterior
and a translucent dark green interior which is so dark as to appear on
casual inspection as black. This is another type of "Cornaline
d'Aleppo" bead.

The two yellow beads are about as different as any two beads could
be. One is a bright yellow seed bead of the usual type A shape, while
the other is a unique, multifaceted translucent specimen belonging to
type H. This bead, which is thick in the center and tapers abruptly
toward each end, has 23 separate facets and is the most intricate
specimen in the collection.

The red beads, of which there are seven belonging to type A, are
really more of a wine color and are all translucent.

Two interesting and unusual beads are blue-lined white with
alternate green and purple stripes painted on them. These stripes
appear to have been applied with a fine tipped brush, a delicate task
since both specimens are only slightly over 2 mm. in diameter.

Of the 20 black beads, 14 belong to type A and 6 to type B. There
is one seed bead of the latter type, but the others are not distinguished
by any unusual characteristics.

Glass beads were assigned definite trade values by the trader or
fur company dealing with a particular group or tribe. The beads
themselves were sent into the field packaged in different ways. Some
were sold in bulk, by the pound, and were shipped in casks, barrels,
or boxes, while others were strung. Stringing was particularly true
of the smaller varieties. The larger varieties were used in necklaces

and for other objects of personal adornment, or were sewn as fringes on garments. The small varieties, particularly the seed type, were intended for sewn beadwork designs. Today only seed beads are sold to the Indians and Eskimos of Alaska and, as previously mentioned, these come packaged in glass tubes.

From a diagnostic standpoint, the most important type of bead in the collection is a form known to the trade as "Cornaline d'Aleppo," so named because it was associated in the Italian export business with the city of Aleppo in Syria. This type of bead is found widely distributed throughout the North American continent and was particularly popular among Indians who traded at the Hudson's Bay Company posts. In fact, this type of bead became known as "Hudson's Bay beads" in regions covered by the Company, and it is probable that independent traders helped to popularize this form in areas peripheral to the Company's posts (Orchard, 1929, p. 87; Woodward, 1959; 1960).

The dark-green-lined red "Cornaline d'Aleppo" is apparently the earliest type and occurs extensively on sites of the 17th and 18th centuries in the Eastern United States and Canada. The white-lined red form is thought to be a more recent type, and at least one authority believes that beads of this kind were confined to the northwestern trade (Orchard, 1929, p. 87). Watkins examined white-lined red beads from the Taral site but was only able to say that the type occurs fairly early in the contact period in the northern Great Plains area (VanStone, 1955, p. 122). It seems likely that both forms of "Cornaline d'Aleppo" bead were introduced into Alaska after extensive use elsewhere in North America, but the exact time of their appearance cannot be determined without further detailed research.

Another type of bead from the Crow Village collection that deserves special attention is the faceted deep-marine-blue bead. The question that arises is whether these are examples of the so-called "Russian beads" which have been found on Russian sites in Alaska as well as along the coast of British Columbia and as far south as Washington and Oregon. Woodward (1959; 1960) has noted that these beads are called "Russian" in spite of the fact that original packages wrapped in gray paper and marked "Brussels" were found unopened in a warehouse of the Russian-American Company at Sitka in 1867. Blue faceted Russian beads are generally large and covered with many small facets, which would make them both larger and more ornate than the Crow Village specimens. This was certainly true of examples examined by VanStone in the collection of the Alaska Historical Library and Museum. On the other hand, Herrick (1957, pl. 5, 51) illustrates blue faceted beads that are identical to the Crow Village specimens, and these were purchased from Indians at Skagway.

By way of summary, it can be said that although precise dating
of the beads from the Crow Village site is not possible, they presumably represent a late 19th-century assemblage of European- and
Syrian-made beads, most of which were used extensively in the North
American trade before being introduced into Alaska. At the same
time, it is at least possible that the blue faceted beads can be identified
as a specific aspect of the Russian trade and would therefore belong
to the period of early contact at Crow Village, a phase which termi-
nated in 1867.

## METAL

Objects of metal form a large and important category of imported
manufactured goods from the Crow Village site. For guidance in
describing and analyzing these materials, particularly the nails, tin
cans, and metallic cartridge cases, we relied heavily on the chapter
concerning metal artifacts in Fontana and Greenleaf (1962). The
reader is referred to this pioneer study in 19th-century historical archeology for informative background material concerning the manufactures described below.

## NAILS

Considering the abundance of metal objects in the collection, it
comes as something of a surprise to find that only 18 nails were recovered. Twelve of these are modern wire nails, the common variety
in use at the present time. About 1855, machines were invented in
France to make complete wire nails automatically. A few of these
were exported to the United States but soon were replaced by similar
machines of American manufacture. By about 1890, machine-made
wire nails were outselling cut nails, and by 1900 the latter type was
made only for special purposes (Fontana and Greenleaf, 1962, p. 55).
All of the wire nails from the site were found embedded in pieces of
cut wood, probably parts of crates or boxes.

The remaining six nails from the site are of the square cut variety,
and each one is a different size. Four are corroded heavily, and five
show indications of having been clinched. The six sizes, expressed
in pennyweights, are as follow: 2d (pl. 14, *j*); 3d (pl. 14, *i*); 5d (pl.
14, *h*); 7d; 10d; 30d. The square cut nail was invented by a New
Englander in 1775, and until about 1810 these nails were headed by a
single hand-driven hammer blow. Between 1810 and 1830 machines
for making square cut nails were perfected until they could produce a
nail that was uniformly cut and headed. A final innovation in the
square cut nail manufacturing process was annealing. After about
1871, cut nails were heated and then slowly cooled to soften and
toughen them at the same time, thus enabling them to be clinched
without rupturing. Fontana and Greenleaf believe that any cut

nail which has been ruptured in bending dates from before 1870. On the strength of this it is possible to say that the five bent Crow Village cut nails, none of which shows signs of rupturing, are post 1870 (Fontana and Greenleaf, 1962, pp. 53–55).

All six of the square cut nails from Crow Village belong to the form called common cut. Common cut nails, used more than any other form of square cut nail, were made in sizes 2d to 60d. All specimens regardless of size have beveled shanks, and all shanks are rectangular in cross section at the point. Common cut nails were used in sheathing, siding and framing with the smaller sizes also being used in boxes and crates (Fontana and Greenleaf, 1962, p. 57). It may have been that most of the nails available to the people of Crow Village had to be removed from boxes.

## TIN CANS

Although can fragments were found extensively throughout the Crow Village site, the quantity and variety of recovered identifiable cans is not great. It will be remembered, however, that can metal was used extensively for the manufacture of artifacts. Many cans and can fragments were discarded in the field, a fact that in retrospect is unfortunate. Although most of the discarded cans were too fragmentary to be identified, an examination of the field notes indicates that seven more or less complete specimens were thrown away, and only two may now be identified from the notes. Had we fully realized the importance of cans at the time of excavation all fragments and complete specimens would have been saved.

With regard to the structure of tin cans and their chronological significance, two important points are to be kept in mind. After the invention of the canning process early in the 19th century, cans were made by hand cutting tin-plated steel. The body of the can was formed around a cylinder and the seam soldered, while separate pieces for the top and bottom also were cut and soldered. A hole was left in the top to insert the food product, and a smaller cap was soldered in place after the can had been filled. A pinhole in the cap would allow gasses to vent, and this could be sealed with a drop of solder as the last step in the process. This type of can became known to the trade as the "hole-in-top," and its construction continued to be improved and was automatic by the 1880's. This method of closure persisted until the early 1900's. The second major innovation in the construction of tin cans was the development of the modern open top can. This development depended on the invention of suitable machines for forming and rolling a hermetic double seam, and the diagnostic feature of this type of can is the locked and lapped seam on the side. By 1902 the old hole-in-top can was being replaced by the newer type,

although it was some time before the new one received general accept-
ance in the industry (Fontana and Greenleaf, 1962, pp. 68–73).

Eleven types of cans from the Crow Village site are identifiable
with some degree of certainty. None of them has the dimensions of the
modern double-seamed cans, nor is it possible to refer any of them to a
specific size of the earlier soldered hole-in-top can. Nevertheless, it
is possible to obtain some idea of the kinds of canned products favored
by and available to the Eskimos.

*Type 1.*—A single rectangular soldered hole-in-top can, nearly
complete but badly corroded, with approximate dimensions of 7.8
by 15.5 cm. This resembles a corned-beef or other meat can of a type
that was extremely popular in the 1880–90 period and frequently is
found around old campsites. The familiar tapered corned-beef can
is similar in construction (Fontana and Greenleaf, 1962, p. 77).

*Type 2.*—A round soldered hole-in-top can 7.5 cm. in diameter and
8.4 cm. in height. This is probably a common fruit or vegetable can.

*Type 3.*—A double-seamed can, badly corroded and of approximately the same dimensions as type 2 but with a central opening 1.8
cm. in diameter at one end. Although small, this should be considered
as a general purpose can, doubtless one of the earliest examples of the
double seamed type.

*Type 4.*—A single double-seamed can 10 cm. in diameter and approximately 12 cm. in height. This general purpose can has an opening
6 cm. in diameter in one end with indications of solder around the edge.
In addition to the nearly complete specimen, there are two end sections
of similar size and shape, both with encrustations of solder around
the openings.

*Type 5.*—A double seamed 5-pound lard pail, badly corroded, was
discarded in the field. Also recovered were the tops of five similar
pails of the same size. All are the same as modern lard pails purchased
by Eskimos today in the Northern Commercial Company store at
Aniak.

*Type 6.*—Two almost complete oblong, soldered sardine cans
approximately 10.7 by 7.5 cm. These are of the roll-top variety and
are probably domestic since foreign fish tins usually are stamped with
the name of the country of origin. This type of can is an important
diagnostic feature of 19th-century sites since the key method of rolling
a scored strip and thus opening the can was invented in 1895 (Fontana
and Greenleaf, 1962, p. 71).

*Type 7.*—This type is represented by the lids of four baking powder
cans. Three of these are from 1-pound cans and the fourth from a
half-pound can. On three of the lids it is possible to determine the
maker's name. In the center of the single half-pound specimen and
on one of the 1-pound can lids the name "Royal Baking Powder" is

present. Around the outside edge above the trade name are the words "full weight" and in a similar position below the trade name the words "absolutely pure." Just above the trade name in the center is the designation "½ lb." In the center of a 1-pound can lid is a crescent moon with the words "trade mark" within the arms of the crescent. Around the outside of the lid is the maker's name, "Crescent Baking Powder." None of these lids is of the screw type, and presumably they all fitted over a cardboard container, presumably with a metal bottom. Royal Baking Powder was introducted in 1866 (Standard Brands), and the Crescent Baking Powder Company was incorporated in 1888 (Belanger, 1963).

*Type 8.*—A single cannisterlike lid is 7.5 cm. in diameter and has a raised screw top opening 3.7 cm. in diameter in the center. This is possibly a fragment of a can for oil, syrup, molasses, or some similar substance.

*Type 9.*—Five tops or bottoms, slightly curved in cross section, are possibly from tobacco cans with hinged covers similar to modern 1½-ounce models. However, all of these specimens have a single hole, approximately 1.2 cm. in diameter, directly in the middle.

*Type 10.*—One specimen is complete, and two tops of small round cans measure 3.9 cm. in diameter. If the single complete can is typical, they stand 1.7 cm. in height. These small cans presumably contained percussion caps for use with cap-lock guns. On one of the lids is the name "Eley Bro.," and below that the word "London." This is the name of a British firm which manufactured percussion caps in the 19th century and is still in business (Russell, 1962, p. 243). The lids of these cans fitted tightly over a slightly constricted rim.

*Type 11.*—This type is represented by a single top fragment, and the shape of the can is unknown. However, it definitely contained some granular material, probably salt, as there are a series of small holes arranged in the shape of a star through which the material would be poured out. A round disk with similar holes is fastened to the lid and could be revolved to close the openings.

As previously indicated, can fragments were found extensively throughout the site, a total of 60 being counted and discarded in the field. Most of these were badly corroded and too fragmentary to indicate the size, shape, or method of manufacture of the cans.

## MISCELLANEOUS

In keeping with the relatively few indications of the use of firearms at Crow Village, only eight *cartridges* were recovered. Four of these are .22-caliber long rifle cartridges which have been drilled at one end for stringing with beads and have been described previously. Since all have been drilled through the proximal end, the maker's marks, if present, have been obliterated. The Colt firearms manufacturers patented the .22-caliber rifle in 1883 and began production in 1888 (Serven, 1960, pp. 361–363), while a Winchester model was first in production in 1884 (Williamson, 1952, p. 424).

There are two .44-caliber rimfire cartridges without manufacturer's marks, presumably for use in Henry's Repeating Rifle. This efficient rimfire rifle was patented in 1860 and manufactured in Winchester's New Haven Arms Company in New Haven, Conn. This cartridge also could have been used in the Model 1866 Winchester or in several single-shot rifles (Fontana and Greenleaf, 1962, p. 81; Smith, 1960, p. 234).

A single center-fire cartridge case with the letters "W.R.A. Co." and "44 WCF" on the head was doubtless used in a Winchester lever action rifle. The .44–.40 center-fire caliber first was used in the famous Model 1873 (Bowman, 1958, pp. 83–84).

The eighth and last cartridge case has the letters "UMC" on the headstamp and the caliber designation "45–70." Also occurring on the head are the letters "S" at 9 o'clock and "H" at 3 o'clock. This caliber cartridge was developed by the United States Army for its own use in the 1870's and was fired in single shot Springfield rifles. The Union Metallic Cartridge Company, the manufacturer of this particular cartridge case, was organized in 1867 in Bridgeport, Conn. Since the firm was merged with the Remington Arms Company in 1910, it is possible to say that this case was made sometime between these two dates (Karr and Karr, 1951, p. 7).

With the exception of the .22-caliber cartridge cases, all other cases are for use in high-powered rifles of the sort that would be used for the hunting of caribou and other big game. It would seem that the rifles represented are late 19th-century prototypes of models in use at the present time.

A blue enameled *teakettle,* a sheet iron *frying pan,* a flat bottomed *iron bucket* with handle, and a *pie tin,* each in a poor state of preservation, were discarded in the field. In addition, three kettle fragments and six bucket sections, all from specimens similar to the complete ones just mentioned, were recovered. Two *kettle lids* seem to have been used with somewhat smaller specimens and presumably were fitted with wooden knob handles (pl. 14, *l*). The collection of household equipment also includes a badly corroded and unmarked *teaspoon* (pl. 14, *f*), a large *serving spoon* with a suspension hole at the extreme end of the handle, the bowl of a *tablespoon,* the handle of a *dipper,* a small copper *hinge* (pl. 14, *r*), and five fragments which are probably from *cast iron stoves.* One of these fragments is large, rounded, and appears to be part of a stove door.

A *wedge* made from a heavy, rectangular piece of cast iron has been pounded flat at the distal end and provided with a spatulate-shaped working edge (pl. 14, *c*). A well made *planing adz blade* also has been constructed from a rectangular bar of cast iron (pl. 14, *b*). It is possible that these artifacts were constructed by Eskimos at the site, but it is doubtful whether heat of sufficient intensity for making such implements could be obtained locally.

There are two single bitted *ax heads*, both with fragmentary cotton-wood handles still in place. The largest specimen is made of steel and is 15.8 cm. in length, 6.5 cm. wide at the butt end, and flares slightly at the working edge. The other implement is of iron and has all the earmarks of having been hand forged. It is battered badly at the butt end suggesting use as a wedge. An examination of both sides of the haft opening reveals narrow lines that suggest the metal initially was two pieces which were molded together. Another interesting feature of this ax head is that it was hafted upside down (pl. 14, *g*). The collection of metal tools also includes a *strike-a-light* (pl. 14, *p*), a heavy *brass spike* used as a chisel (pl. 14, *e*), and a narrower *iron spike* that may have been similarly used (pl. 14, *d*).

Two *buckles* that were used on clothing were recovered. One of these (pl. 14, *g*), stamped "Shirley" and "PAT. AUG. 23. 92" was used with a pair of men's suspenders. The other (pl. 14, *m*) is of the type that may have been used to secure overall straps. Also included are a narrow copper *bracelet* (pl. 14, *o*) and an interesting *pendant*, also of copper, for the most part round but flat across the bottom and stamped with a rosette design (pl. 14, *n*).

The remaining metal objects are *unidentified iron scraps*, a *bayonet fragment* (pl. 14, *a*), and a single *unidentified iron object* which is narrow, rectangular, and rounded at both ends, with what appears to be a suspension hole drilled at one end (pl. 14, *k*).

## WOOD

Only a very small number of imported wooden objects were found at Crow Village, and none of them is complete. Two *box fragments* are both rectangular but differ greatly in size. One is relatively heavy and is probably one end of a large box. It measures 37.0 by 14.5 by 1.9 cm. and has been used extensively as a cutting board. Seven wire nails have been driven into the sides. The other is small and light, measuring 11.8 by 5.8 cm. and looks very much like the end of a cigarbox. Five small headless wire nails project from this specimen. Other imported wooden objects are a single *barrel stave* 32 cm. in length and two knife handle fragments, presumably of the kind associated with the common kitchen *paring knife*.

## Textiles and Footwear

Although the Eskimos at Crow Village undoubtedly obtained a variety of American clothing, there is little indication from recovered textile material of the range of types available to them. Nor is it possible to say to what extent woven textiles were replacing traditional Eskimo clothing since no remains of the latter were found. From the six textile fragments in the collection, only two items of clothing can be recognized. One of these is a black wide-brimmed *hat* of a heavily-felted woven woolen material, and the other is a square *kerchief* of Chinese silk. Both are in a very poor state of preservation. In addition, there is a small brown fragment of a similar material that was probably originally red, as well as one green and two small black fragments that are also the same but not as heavily felted. These are possibly fragments of coats.

Footwear is represented in the collection by three specimens: the sole and heel of a man's rubber *overshoe*, the similar parts of a *man's square-toed shoe*, and an almost complete *woman's laced boot*. Unfortunately there is nothing diagnostic about the overshoe fragment, but the section of the man's shoe is more revealing. On the latter specimen the inner and outer soles have been fastened together with headless brass nails driven along the outer edges, probably by a machine. Although the top of the sole is missing, portions of the upper leather remain where it has been tacked between the inner and outer soles by a series of iron tackets. In 1858 a machine was invented that would sew the sole of a shoe to the upper part with thread, but how long after that tackets and other metal fasteners continued to be used it is impossible to determine (Fontana and Greenleaf, 1962, pp. 103–105). However, it seems unlikely that the shoe under discussion was made before 1860. The woman's laced boot is of similar construction and thus would seem to be about the same age. After an examination of the boot, Harold Burnham, a clothing authority at the Royal Ontario Museum, observed that if it had been found in southern Ontario, he would be inclined to date it in the 1860's.

## Miscellaneous

The final item of imported material is an irregular *lump of tar* which may have been used in the construction and repair of boat coverings. Since tar would probably not be particularly satisfactory as a material for the repair of skin coverings, it is probable that the substance would have been used with canvas or even birchbark.

## CONTINUITY AND INNOVATION

Recovering sociocultural and other remains from a site where ethnographic and historical information is available gives an added dimension to the usual archeological inferences. In this context, under favorable circumstances a single site excavation can provide an exceptionally large amount of information about the processes of sociocultural stability and change. Seemingly the Crow Village site represents such a pleasing combination. From history we know that the community was occupied in 1844 and that the last occupants left between 1906 and 1912. Furthermore, it is clear that the village residents represented the farthest inland settlement of the Yuk in early historical times. History provides this outline and more, while ethnography offers another kind of information. The ethnography of most value was compiled by Edward W. Nelson (1899) for the Eskimos of western Alaska. Nelson's descriptions are of materials for both Yuk and Inuit speaking peoples. Fortunately for this study, he collected a great deal of data for the area from St. Michael southward to the Kuskokwim River mouth. Thus he provided a description of the historic coastal Eskimo culture which, in its prehistoric form, was the basis out of which riverine Eskimo culture along the Kuskokwim grew.

A comparison of the Nelson collection with a historic and recent prehistoric archeological collection from Hooper Bay Village (Oswalt, 1952) suggests that Nelson's material represents a norm for aboriginal central Bering Sea coast Eskimo technology for the historic and recent prehistoric eras. It is apparent that the Crow Village collection is within the tradition of coastal Yuk culture. In spite of certain special characteristics, there can be no doubt that the inhabitants of Crow Village possessed a material culture that was not radically different from that of their coastal kin. This fact is illustrated graphically when the Crow Village artifacts are compared with the materials collected by Nelson and those excavated by Oswalt at Hooper Bay Village. Very briefly, such a comparison reveals that an overwhelming majority of the traditional artifacts in all categories can be duplicated in one or the other of these collections. The similarity is particularly evident when the wooden artifacts from Crow Village are considered. This is not only the largest category of artifacts but is the most revealing culturally as well as the most comparable, particularly with regard to the collection made by Nelson. Of the nearly 250 identifiable traditional wooden objects, only seven forms are not present in the Nelson collection. These are the "lance" fragment, the wooden fish spear side prong, bench plank support, checker, flip dart, segmented doll, and "flat" carving. None of these forms is particularly diagnostic, and in some cases identification is tentative.

Thus the Crow Village collection of indigenous manufactured goods accurately reflects 19th-century coastal Bering Sea Eskimo material culture. The latter Eskimos possessed a cultural inventory which was not only elaborate but also diversified in its forms, particularly with reference to the economic sphere. They had a technology well adapted to sea mammal hunting, hunting and trapping on the land, and taking fish. These people could readily adjust their economic lives to any situation compatible with their existing technology. This seems to be precisely what happened when they entered the Kuskokwim River system. Fishing and land hunting methods were emphasized and sea mammal hunting forgotten. In light of the similarities between Bering Sea coast and Crow Village artifact forms, it seems likely that either the Yuk movement inland was (1) quite recent; (2) early but retentive of close ties with the coastal peoples, or; (3) a combination of both situations. In any of these interpretations the basic cultural continuity is clear.

Even within the context of historical contact, there is additional and more specific evidence of continuity with the past. Traditional Eskimo stoneworking continued but with a different emphasis. Hammerstones existed because of their general efficiency as multipurpose pounding implements, but they were not as plentiful as might be expected, judging from their number and diversity in recent coastal Eskimo sites. Whetstones on the other hand were numerous, and since they would function to sharpen stone or metal blades and needles their continuity was assured. Their diversity of quality was probably a function of the different qualities of stone necessary for sharpening either stone or metal. Likewise stone-bladed ulus were frequently recovered. In light of the presence of similar blade forms made from can metal, which could not have functioned effectively, we infer that large pieces of metal suitable for ulu blades were unavailable. Even if such metal had been available, it is doubtful that sufficient skill would have existed to refashion the metal into an ulu blade. Today (1963) ulu blades are cut from old wood-saw blades, and it requires good tools as well as knowledge of reworking metal to produce a serviceable ulu. Perhaps the most striking evidence of continuity in stone technology is found in stone artifacts for working skins. There is a greater diversity of these types than in any other stone category. This leads to the assumption that the technology of the Russians and Anglo-Americans could not contribute to this complex. An alternative explanation would be that the women were simply conservative in their skinworking techniques, but we favor the former reason.

Probably the most striking characteristic of Crow Village material culture is the continuity of wooden artifact forms. This point has previously been made but merits repeating. As long as the site was occupied, the traditional woodworking technology persisted and most forms continued. Metal tools unquestionably increased the efficiency of woodworking, but they did not change its character nor did new wooden forms of the Russians or Anglo-Americans make a deep impression. Most wooden artifacts can be identified in terms of the traditional forms.

An examination of the trait list (Appendix 1) illustrates that from the T–1 midden proportionally more objects of wood were recovered than artifacts of any other material. Particularly noticeable is the scarcity of trade goods and household equipment from the T–1 midden, in contrast with the relative abundance of these objects in the T–2 midden. The association of the T–1 midden with the working of wood is reinforced by the fact that an overwhelming majority of the unidentified fragments of worked wood recovered from the site came from there. This is not particularly surprising when it is realized that this midden is located directly in front of the *kashgee*, while T–2 is at the entrances to H–3 and H–4. Thus the objects recovered from T–2 are associated with domestic rubbish, while those from T–1 represent the wood manufactures that would be likely to take place in the *kashgee*.

One of the most striking features of the excavation was the scarcity of bone and antler both from the houses and middens. A table of bone occurrences, in which the bones are not distinguished between left and right (table 2), is quite revealing. It is more than chance that only one bone was recovered from the extensive T–1 midden. When bones were comparatively plentiful, as the beaver bones from T–2, they could be associated with a single animal. It might be inferred that the animals represented in the bone collection were rare in the locality and seldom hunted, yet this seems highly unlikely from the comments by Zagoskin (1956, pp. 204, 220–221) and informants' statements (Oswalt, 1963 b, pp. 127–128). The scarcity of bones is understandable only in the context of statements by informants. When Oswalt asked Sam Phillips about the situation in 1953 and Anania Theodore in 1954, both stated that animal bones were thrown into the river to prevent the dogs from chewing them. It was thought that for dogs to chew bones would offend the spirit of the animal involved and, as a consequence, the species would be difficult if not impossible to take in the future. This belief and its practice is partially validated by the absence of bones chewed by dogs although dogs were represented in the collection of bones. If the Crow Village site were not in a historical context, the absence of bones probably would be considered as in some way associated with a supernatural involvement making it necessary to deposit the bones outside of the

TABLE 2.—*Animal bones recovered from the site*

| Animal bone | House | | | | | Test trench | | |
|---|---|---|---|---|---|---|---|---|
| | 1 | 2 | 3 | 4 | 5 | 1 | 2 | 3 |
| Beaver (*Castor canadensis canadensis*): | | | | | | | | |
| Cranium | | | | | | | 1 | |
| Mandible | | | 1 | 3 | | | 5 | |
| Incisors | | | | | | | 2 | |
| Pelvic bone | | | | | | 1 | 1 | |
| Humerus | | | | 2 | | | | |
| Caribou (*Rangifer stonei*): | | | | | | | | |
| Scapula | | | | 3 | | | | |
| Humerus, proximal end | | | | 1 | | | | |
| Humerus, distal end | 1 | | 1 | | | | | |
| Ulna, proximal end | | | 2 | | | | | |
| Ulna, distal end | | | 2 | | | | | |
| Ribs | 4 | | 1 | | | | | |
| Vertebra | | | 1 | | | | | |
| Metacarpal | | | 1 | | | | | |
| Pelvic bone | | | 1 | | | | | |
| Astragalus | | | 1 | | | | | |
| Metatarsal | | | 1 | | | | | |
| Femur | | | 1 | | | | | |
| Dog (*Canis familiaris*): | | | | | | | | |
| Skeleton without skull | | | 1 | | | | | |
| Skeleton, partial | 1 | 1 | | | | | | |
| Cranium | | | | 1 | | | | |
| Mandible | 2 | 2 | 1 | 1 | 1 | | | |
| Maxillary fragment | | | 1 | | | | | |
| Scapula | 1 | | 1 | | | | | |
| Radius | | | | | | 1 | | |
| Humerus | 2 | | 2 | | | | | |
| Femur | | | 2 | | | | | |
| Pelvic bone | | | 1 | | | | | |
| Hare (*Lepus americanus macfarlani*): | | | | | | | | |
| Skull | 1 | | | | | | 1 | |
| Humerus | 1 | | | | | | 1 | |
| Scapula | 1 | | | | | | | |
| Femur | | | | | | | 1 | |
| Pelvic bone | 2 | | | | | | | |
| Tibia | 4 | | | | | | | |
| Moose (*Alces gigas*): | | | | | | | | |
| Mandible | | | 3 | | | | | |
| Scapula | 1 | | 1 | | | | | |
| Humerus | | | 2 | 1 | | | | |
| Ulna | 1 | | | | | | 1 | |
| Tibia, proximal end | | | 1 | | | | | |
| Femur, proximal end | | | | | 1 | | | |
| Femur, distal end | 1 | | | | | | | |
| Tibia | | 2 | 2 | | | | | |
| Vertebra | | | 2 | | | | | |
| Metatarsal | | 1 | | | 1 | | | |
| Red fox (*Vulpes alascensis alascensis*): | | | | | | | | |
| Mandible | | | 2 | | | | | |
| Pelvic bone | 1 | | | | | | | |
| Squirrel (*Citellus osgoodi*): | | | | | | | | |
| Cranium | 2 | | | 1 | | | | |
| Mandible | | | 1 | | | | | |

site. This is of course precisely what informants revealed. The absence of chewed bones, however, might be overlooked and the association with dogs not drawn.

We were rather surprised at the presence of moose bones and their greater frequency than caribou bones. Informants and the sketchy historical records both lead us to believe that moose were rare along the central Kuskokwim until within the past 30 years. If these sources are correct then the moose bones must represent animals hunted at a considerable distance upstream from Crow Village. This is not unlikely since fur trapping brought about upriver penetration by central river people (Oswalt, 1963 b, p. 129).

The frequencies of dog bones are both revealing and puzzling. Considering the three partial dog skeletons and other dog bones, there were more bones of this species represented than any other. It is interesting also that mandibles of dogs were found in every house, and in three houses (H–2, –4, –5) very few other bones were present. Noteworthy too is the presence of partially articulated dog skeletons in three separate dwellings (H–1, –2, –3). It is tempting to regard dog bones as having special significance, but the precise meaning of this fact, if it is a fact, is obscure.

In spite of the scarcity of caribou bones, there are artifacts made from antler, a fact which suggests the hunting of this animal. Antler artifacts, however, are not plentiful although conditions for their preservation were favorable. Continuity with the past and with coastal Eskimos is much less obvious in the antlerworking technology than it is with reference to woodworking. In totality it seems that caribou were hunted but were not very important, while antler was replaced partially by wood or nonaboriginal materials.

The use of bone in the manufacture of artifacts is extremely rare at Crow Village. Bone is not a particularly desirable substance out of which to make artifacts since its overall surface is small and it is quite brittle. It is especially undesirable if antler is available. The only artifacts made from locally available bone were a net sinker and awls. A ramrod and sled shoe, both of whalebone, must have been received from the coast in trade. Considering the boneworking emphasis of the Northern Athapaskans and the nearness of the Crow Village people to these Indians, there is no evidence of any borrowing of boneworking ideas.

As has been seen, the mammal bones discussed thus far give a distorted picture of the species taken. This is also likely regarding the fur-bearing animals. In a record of the fur pelts traded into Kolmakov Redoubt between the years 1845 and 1860, with the exception of 1857 (Petroff, 1884, pp. 62–65), we find that beaver were numerically by far the most important, then red fox, land otter, lynx, and bear.  From 1856 to the end of the record, marten became extremely important.  In the American period for the year 1883 we have a record of all the furs traded to the Alaska Commercial Company at their three stores: Mumtreklagamiut Station (Bethel), Kolmakov, and Vinasale.  Numerically the most important pelt was the muskrat, then mink, followed by marten, beaver, fox, land otter, and black bear (Oswalt, 1963 b, pp. 109–110).  It was only by exchanging pelts for trade goods that an Eskimo could obtain those exotic items which he desired.  The Crow Village people unquestionably were participants in the fur trade, and yet there is little evidence of the species that they took.  A few beaver bones were associated with H–3, H–4, and T–2, but again we would expect beaver and other species to be represented more widely in the site, were it not known that bones were thrown into the river.  According to informants, fishbones also were thrown into the river.  During the excavation a few scales and vertebrae from fish were recovered, but these were only a minute fraction of the number that would be expected at a riverine site where fishing was a major, if not *the* major, means of livelihood.

Zagoskin (1956, p. 221) mentions that metal traps were unsuccessfully introduced for the trapping of beaver and that the aboriginal trapping methods for taking this animal persisted, with the additional Russian technique of destroying the beaver's lodge.  Eskimo-made traps, consisting of snares, nets, deadfalls, and so on, would not only be unlikely to leave traces in the archeological record, but would, in in any case, be set at some distance from the village and discarded when broken or worn out.  It will be remembered, however, that there are some small wooden pegs in the collection that have tentatively been identified as snare parts.  The significance of trapping to the Crow Village people and its effect on the annual subsistence cycle will be discussed elsewhere.  Here it is sufficient to say that the absence from the collection of artifacts related to trapping does not necessarily indicate a lack of emphasis on this activity.

The birchbark technology at the site does not represent a development from coastal Eskimo material culture; birchbark in that area was recovered only from driftwood and through trade.  Thus a case cannot be made for continuity, but working birchbark seems to represent a new development induced by a new environmental setting plus the probability of borrowings from the Athapaskans.  The prevalence of birchbark in the site in the form of baskets, storage pit liners, roof log coverings, and floor coverings, plus innumerable unworked fragments, already has been noted.  In fact, it is difficult to escape the conclusion that the preparation of birchbark for its various uses must have been an important activity.  The effect that the prevalence of birchbark vessels may have had on the scarcity of traditional pottery is discussed elsewhere. It is significant, too, that grass matting usually associated with the Eskimos of southwestern Alaska is virtually absent from the site, and its replacement by birchbark is likely. It is interesting to note that all the fragments of worked birchbark were recovered from the T–1 midden, suggesting that baskets and other objects of this material may have been made by the men in the *kashgee*. This explanation would not, however, be consistent with the present day situation as baskets are now made by the women.

Working clay into containers within the tradition of potterymaking is seen in its last stage at the site. The fragments of imported pottery outnumber those of the locally made ware. It is true, too, that a preference for birchbark containers may be responsible partially for the scarcity of clay vessels. The use of clay cooking pots was in rapid decline, but lamps continued to be useful, as indicated by 15 pottery lamp fragments, the 2 sections of imported stone lamps, and the lampstands in two houses. While imported pottery and birchbark containers could easily replace clay pots, there seems to have been no satisfactory substitute for the traditional Eskimo lamp. This is likely to have been due to the scarcity of imported fuel, rather than a failure on the part of the Eskimos to appreciate the advantages of the kerosene or coal oil lamp.

Having considered those features of Crow Village culture in which continuity with the past is certain, likely, or vague, it is now fitting to deal with the instances of change induced by the contact situation. This is the realm in which we would expect "ingenuity" to be most evident. We have come to expect Eskimos to innovate along technological lines and to be original in manipulating new things; the evidence at the site supports this generalization. An inspection of the list of imported manufactured goods suggests that a relatively small number of trade items were available to the people throughout the period represented by the site. It is not the actual numbers or variety of the imported items that is impressive, but rather the manner in which imported material was adapted to local needs. In fact, it is important that the inhabitants of Crow Village frequently remade trade items into new things, while items from the traditional culture rarely were remade. This is striking, since the secondary use of artifacts is a characteristic of Eskimo material culture from prehistoric sites.

It is the stimulus toward innovation provided by the exposure to new and different forms that is most impressive. In situations where innovations occur as a result of contact we would expect things new to arise from: (1) exotic objects introduced, accepted, and added to the

cultural inventory without formal changes; (2) the availability of new
materials permitting a change of existing forms; and (3) the construction of new forms based on new models.   With regard to the first
source of innovation, a reading of the artifact descriptions and a
glance at the trait list will indicate which items were accepted into
the cultural inventory without change.   The impression is that the
process of selection was not a complex one.   Relatively few items
appear to have been available, and they pertained to aspects of
culture in which one might expect that innovation would be the least
disruptive and the most acceptable: new forms of tools, weapons,
household equipment, and items of clothing and ornamentation.   Of
particular interest are those items which indicate the introduction
of new foods.   The cans recovered point to the use of the following
food products: meat, fruit, lard, fish, baking powder, syrup or oil,
tobacco, and salt.   We can assume that tea was obtained either in
bricks or in packages that would leave no trace.   The food products
represented here are among the most popular with Kuskokwim
Eskimos today.   Baking powder and lard are used in making bannock
and are considered staples, while canned meats and fruit are luxuries.
It then appears that a desire for these imported food products was
established at an early date in the middle Kuskokwim region, but only
tea can be traced through historical references to the Russian period.

Of far greater interest and significance is the second source of
innovation.   Here we are concerned with the introduction of new
materials and their effect on the construction of traditional artifact
types and the persistence of old ideas in new mediums.   The most
notable examples are discussed below.

(1) *The drilled mending hole in a sherd of imported pottery* is the application of an
old technique for mending traditional Eskimo pottery to the new imported pottery.
Presumably this transference was reasonably successful, although imported pottery breaks with a straight edge that would make successful mending by this means
very difficult.

(2) *Ulu blades from can metal* were doubtless easier to make and could be constructed more quickly in larger sizes than those made of stone.   However, the
flexible nature of the metal and its inability to hold an edge must have made these
blades less useful than those of stone.   The fact that certain other tools were made
from can metal and that can metal was cut and stored in rolls suggests that the
people were experimenting with its uses.

(3) *The salmon dart head of metal* represents no radical change in design and might
just as easily have been made in the traditional way from antler.   Here is an
excellent example of an old and familiar artifact type reproduced in a new material
without reference to the specific qualities of that material.

(4) *Scrapers made from bottle glass* are in no way different in overall form from
those made of flinty materials.   Given the presence of heavy bottle glass, the
scrapers must have been more easily manufactured and at the same time provided
a use for broken bottles.

(5) *The use of a spent cartridge case to form the end of a bird dart head* is only a slight modification of a traditional artifact, but undoubtedly this change increased the durability of the point.

(6) *The example of can metal folded into shallow dishlike containers* is particularly interesting because it illustrates a conservatism with regard to the new material. The can metal appears to have been viewed as having the same properties as birchbark, and since this is true to some extent, the transition from one material to another was quite successful. While can metal was apparently never plentiful enough, or available in large enough sections, to replace birchbark, the shallow dishes seem to have formed a useful addition to the cultural inventory.

(7) *The use of a nail with the head filed away in place of a bird bone splinter* for the tip of a dart seems to be an innovation whose value would immediately recommend it, involving as it does no change in the shape or design of the traditional form but giving added strength against breakage.

(8) *Twenty-two (.22-) caliber cartridge cases were perforated at the cap and a cord passed through the holes.* The cases were strung with beads and became a new form of necklace.

(9) *The engraved metal ferrule* with encircling lines and short lines at right angles to one of the circles represents making a design in metal which had no aboriginal precedent.

Turning to our third category of innovation, that of new forms based on new models, the number of examples is small. This points up a basic fact about the nature of culture change at Crow Village, namely, that as a result of contact, very few needs were created that could not be fulfilled through the normal trade channels. Thus it was only occasionally necessary for the Eskimos to improvise in order to maintain and continue to use the imported implements which they had already. The most notable example of the attempt to reproduce a non-Eskimo artifact locally is the sandstone bullet mold half. Only one other item seems to fit into this general innovative category, and that is the artifact identified as a wooden flower. This is a form which has no referent in the old culture and may represent a response to the use of flowers in the services of the Russian Orthodox Church.

The various specifics of innovation mentioned above are interesting because of the information they provide about the response of the Eskimos to the introduction of new items of material culture. We note that the people of Crow Village seem to have responded enthusiastically to the relatively small number of imported items which were available to them toward the close of the 19th century, and particularly they seem to have been interested in experimenting with new materials. Although neither the archeological record nor historical material permits us to elaborate on the selection factor and trade materials, it is assumed that the Eskimos of this area accepted whatever was offered. We have the definite impression that the inventory of goods traded into the middle Kuskokwim area during both the Russian and early American periods was not great.

However, the truly impressive characteristic of the Crow Village collection is not the imported goods or their use but rather the remarkable continuity represented, with emphasis on the retention of traditional forms. The fact that traditional Eskimo material cuture should loom as large as it does in this collection from a site that apparently was occupied only during the contact period seems to suggest a single important fact: During the middle and late 19th century, in an area of Alaska exploited by American and Russian traders for three-quarters of a century, Eskimo material culture retained its traditional orientation. When this is considered in light of the change that has taken place in the area since then, it is possible to appreciate the rapidity with which the Eskimos have been drawn into the mainstream of American life since the turn of the century.

## TIME AND CHANGE

The span of time represented at Crow Village is approximately 90 years. The presence of trade goods in the lowest midden levels and throughout the house floors demonstrates that there was at least indirect historic contact during the earliest stages of occupancy. It is highly probable that Russian trade goods were obtained before the Russians entered the river, but it is doubtful that such trade items were plentiful even during the Russian period. After 1867, Americans influenced Crow Village life, both directly and indirectly, until the site was abandoned early in the 20th century. Historical information regarding the Kuskokwim region is scarce, but it is possible to single out particular spans of time and changes which were crucial in the history of the Crow Village Yupik.

### 1818–1829

While Alexandrov Redoubt was being constructed at the mouth of the Nushagak River in 1818, a party on the cutter *Constantine* ascended the Kuskokwim River a short distance but soon returned to the redoubt since the season was late. Here we have direct Russian contact on the Kuskokwim with people who must have been Eskimos (Tikhmenev, 1861, pp. 300–302). Again in 1821 we have a reference to a person from the Kuskokwim visiting Iliamna and the notation that the Kuskokwim people could readily trade at the Nushagak station (Documents Relative History Alaska, vol. 4, pp. 243–244). In 1822 there is a reference to Kuskokwim travelers to Alexandrov (ibid., p. 321), and 11 persons from the Kuskokwim were at the same station in 1830 (Tikhmenev, 1861, p. 340). This series of citations serves to illustrate that Kuskokwim peoples were traveling to the Nushagak River trading center probably both by coastal and inland routes, and unquestionably they returned to their homes with Russian imports.

## 1830–1866

A Russian party under Vasil'ev in 1830 ascended the Nushagak River to a stream flowing into the Kuskokwim. They ascended the Kuskokwim for an unknown distance and then followed the river downstream to the seacoast (Tikhmenev, 1861, pp. 340–341). This exploration was pursued in order to expand the fur trade into the interior of southwestern Alaska, and one of the immediate goals of the trip appears to have been the founding of a Kuskokwim trading station. In 1832 such a post was established at the Holitna and Kuskokwim River junctions. The following year it was abandoned and a new one erected at Kwigiumpainukamiut (Zagoskin, 1956, p. 258; VanStone, 1959, p. 46). The final Russian trading establishment began to function at Kolmakov Redoubt in 1841 (Zagoskin, 1956, p. 258). Subsidiary stores at Ogavik, Vinasale, and Mumtrekhlagamiut Station (modern Bethel) represent the range of known Russian trading posts along the river (for details see Oswalt, 1963 b).

The imported manufactured goods found at Crow Village were analyzed earlier in an attempt to date the various trade items. There is little that can be added on this subject, and we must be content with the general observation that the trade materials, taken as a whole, appear to belong to the latter part of the 19th century. This statement does not, however, answer all questions concerning the matter of dating unless we are prepared to say that all the trade goods from the site belong to the period of American influence, that is, the period after the purchase. Since Crow Village was occupied at the time of Zagoskin's visit to the central Kuskokwim in 1843 and 1844, and presumably for some time before these dates, it is to be expected that materials belonging to the Russian period would occur in the collection. In fact, prior to the excavation of the site, the authors had anticipated that their work would make it possible to arrive at definite conclusions concerning the nature of both Russian and American trade influences. A clear dichotomy did not emerge, and therefore a major problem is to determine which trade goods are of Russian origin and which were obtained from American traders.

In order to answer this question, or at least to make a reasonable attempt at answering it, we must turn to the historical sources, namely Zagoskin. According to him the specific trade goods which the Russians introduced to the Kuskokwim included black and white beads, tobacco, Aleutian axes, copper and cast iron dishes, flannel blankets, and items of European clothing. Other items offered for trade by the Russians in southwestern Alaska, which probably were introduced along the Kuskokwim River, included small white beads, "long" beads, small red and black beads, steel-colored and blue beads, knives, spears of iron, steel for striking a fire, needles, combs, pipes, tin and cast iron pots, large cups, mirrors, copper rings, earrings, small bells, and navy buttons (Zagoskin, 1956, pp. 137, 153, 164, 252–253).

It would be desirable if the list of Russian trade goods was more explicitly descriptive, but this is the only known inventory. It is clear from this list that there are at least a few Russian trade items in the Crow Village collection. Most notable in this regard are the beads. An earlier analysis of the beads stressed the general 19th-century character of the assemblage, although very little was said about the possible origin of the various forms of beads. It was possible to identify with a fair degree of certainty only the faceted blue beads as Russian, but likewise it is true that any European-made bead could have been obtained by the Russians for their Alaskan trade. The difficulty here is that the sale or trading of beads to the Kuskokwim Eskimos has continued right down to the present time. It is undoubtedly true that various shapes, colors, and sizes of beads were traded at specific times, but our knowledge of the bead trade on the Kuskokwim, or anywhere else in Alaska for that matter, is not detailed enough to present a chronology based on bead types. All that can be said is that Zagoskin lists four colors of beads that occur in the Crow Village collection and there is the possibility that these were Russian trade items.

The single copper bracelet in the collection is, with the exception of the beads, the object most likely to be considered as of Russian origin. It is possible that some of the cast iron fragments may be from the types of dishes and pots described by Zagoskin, and the same applies to the iron strike-a-light and knife blade. In spite of the existence of these presumably Russian artifacts, however, it is clear that the bulk of the imported manufactured goods from Crow Village belong to the American period and were obtained from the traders who succeeded those of the Russian-American Company on the Kuskokwim. This can mean only that the Russian influence at Crow Village was slight, at least in terms of material culture, in spite of the nearness of the Kolmakov trading station and the acknowledged influence of the Russian Orthodox Church in the village.

This situation is difficult to understand, and perhaps the only reasonable explanation lies in the reemphasis of a point that has already been made: The actual period of Russian influence along the middle Kuskokwim was not only relatively short but lacked intensity. The rarity of published accounts dating from the Russian occupation makes it difficult to assess the influence the Russians exerted on the lives of the Kuskokwim Eskimos. It has been stated that, initially, the Russians came to the river for the purpose of expanding their inland fur trade. They were few in number, and they appear to have established their role among the people with caution. They had no force to back up their position and thus could not afford to oppose the people as they had been able to do in the Aleutians, on Kodiak Island, and throughout southeastern Alaska. The Russians apparently did not interfere in the affairs of the various Kuskokwim villages with which they had contact, nor did they establish their major trading station in an occupied village (Oswalt, 1963 b, pp. 106–107). Their influence along the Kuskokwim then was minor as far as Eskimo material culture was concerned.

A less tangible result of Russian intervention was the introduction of Christianity to the Kuskokwim peoples. The endeavors of the Russian Orthodox priests were hampered by the inaccessibility of the area, the scattered nature of the Eskimo and Indian settlements, and the physical mobility of the people they hoped to convert. It appears that Father Veniaminov was the first to baptize Eskimos north of the Alaska Peninsula. In 1829 he performed the ritual for 13 individuals at Nushagak, and during a second visit there in 1832 he held church services for 70 persons (Tikhmenev, 1861, pp. 359–360; Barsukov, 1886–88, vol. 2, p. 37). Feodor Kolmakov, after whom Kolmakov Redoubt was named, served at the Nushagak station as a trader and missionary. He participated widely in Kuskokwim and Yukon River explorations and everywhere baptized receptive Eskimos and Indians (Zagoskin, 1956, p. 44; Barsukov, 1886–88, vol. 2, p. 38). As noted previously, when Zagoskin was at Crow Village in 1843, 20 of the 90 residents were regarded as Christians. Two of the Christian families living there recently had moved from Alexandrov Redoubt. In one record it is noted that from June 1850 to the same time of the next year, 203 persons were baptized among the Kuskokwim inhabitants. In general, the missionary working with these people about this time found that those living nearest the mission, Kolmakov Redoubt, were most influenced by his teaching, and we might infer that this would include the Crow Village Eskimos (Barsukov, 1897–1901, vol. 1, pp. 369–370). The already quoted statement of Hieromonk Illarion about the Crow Village Christians is instructive, for obviously these Eskimos poorly understood the nature of Christianity by the end of the Russian era.

Information about the number of people along the central Kuskokwim River within historic times is quite inadequate, but it is possible to learn something of the nature of the settlement pattern. Initially it should be mentioned that immediately prior to the time of the first population statistics for specific villages, there was a smallpox epidemic in southwestern Alaska. It apparently struck the area in 1838–39 (Zagoskin, 1956, pp. 61, 134), and of the 550 persons who contracted the disease at Alexandrov, St. Michael, and along the

Kuskokwim, 200 died (Tikhmenev, 1861, pp. 366–368). This does not
provide a meaningful index to its effect on the Kuskokwim peoples
except to suggest that it did not kill vast numbers of people as might
have been expected. Considering the river area about 60 km. up
and downstream from Crow Village as within the immediate vicinity,
Zagoskin (Petroff, 1884, p. 37) recorded in 1843 or 1844 that Crow
Village had 90 residents living in five houses, the downstream
village of Ohagamiut had 61 persons, and 120 lived slightly farther
downriver at Kalskag. No upriver community is listed until
Kwigiumpainukamiut, which is beyond the 30 km. radius but nonetheless had 89 Eskimo and 71 Athapaskan residents. In light of the
fact that Zagoskin twice visited the central Kuskokwim during his
travels, there is no reason to question the validity of his figures. In
this case we would have a total of 271 persons at Crow Village and
in the vicinity. We do not have comparable statistics available for
the latter part of the Russian period, but we would assume that the
population increased slowly after the smallpox epidemic. In any case
the population of this sector of the central Kuskokwim certainly was
quite small throughout its early history.

1867–1912

The purchase of Alaska by the United States did not change the
basic relationship between the Eskimos and the traders. The succeed-
ing trading enterprise, the Hutchinson, Kohl & Company, which was
soon reorganized as the Alaska Commercial Company, continued to
operate stores at Kolmakov, Vinasale, and Mumtrekhlagamiut
Station, but apparently discontinued the Ogavik station. The
Alaska Commercial Company had competition from the Western
Fur and Trading Company for a brief period, and at least one free
trader operated a store for a short period of time (Oswalt, 1963 b,
pp. 102–132). Precisely what the traders had to offer the people in
terms of material goods is not known in detail. An exhaustive search
has been made of various archives to locate merchandise inventories
for the Kuskokwim River stations. However, it is rather certain that
these records were destroyed in the San Francisco earthquake and fire.
From scattered sources it is possible to piece together an uncertain
picture of the popular trade items in southwestern Alaska during the
earlier phases of American occupancy. E. W. Nelson, when traveling
from St. Michael to the Kuskokwim River mouth in 1878, took "leaf
tobacco, ammunition, beads, brass jewelry, needles and other small
wares" in order to purchase ethnographic materials (Nelson, 1882,
p. 661). In the 1880's the Moravian missionary W. H. Weinland
listed tobacco, tea, drilling (fabric), needles, powder, lead, knives,
axes, hardtack, twine, sugar, flour, and cooking utensils as the most

popular trade items. He mentioned also old Army muskets and sheet
iron teakettles (Oswalt, 1963 b, pp. 110–111). In his unpublished
diary Weinland records that while at Ohagamiut he saw a young
girl wearing a headband and breast ornament which were decorated
with red, blue, and white beads, small and large brass buttons, and
empty brass cartridge cases (Weinland Collection: W. H. Weinland
diary entry for July 1, 1884). Elsewhere in his 1884 account Weinland
mentions that the women wear colored kerchiefs on their heads
(ibid., entry for June 17, 1884). From the descriptions of Kuskokwim
Eskimos by this missionary for the years 1884–87, it is apparent that
the people then possessed the material apparatus of aboriginal
Eskimos with the addition of relatively few trade items.

One trade item which merits particular attention in a historical
context is firearms. It is necessary to account for the scarcity of guns,
gun parts, and other objects associated with firearms at Crow Village.
It will be recalled that there are no recognized gun parts in the collection and relatively few objects associated with guns. It therefore
seems reasonable that guns of any kind were rare and valuable posses-
sions not only during the Russian period but through the early
American period as well. Guns were not used along the Kuskokwim
in 1843–44, as reported by Zagoskin, but they were being used at
Alexandrov and Nicholaevskij redoubts at this time. Zagoskin
suggested in his report that firearms be introduced, but whether this
recommendation was implemented is not known. It is known, however, that powder and lead were among the most important trade
items desired by the Kuskokwim Eskimos in the 1880's, and muskets
were being sold at Kolmakov at this time (Oswalt, 1963 b, pp. 110–
111). Before 1896 there was a United States Government regulation
which prohibited the sale of breech-loading rifles to the Eskimos of
Alaska. Although this law frequently was broken, at least in northwestern Alaska, it is likely to have been more effective in the interior
where the opportunity to purchase rifles, shotguns, and ammunition
from transient individuals presumably was less than along the coast.
As just mentioned, Weinland noted that brass cartridge cases were
used for ornaments, which suggests that breech-loading guns to fire
these shells were present. The Alaska Commercial Company was
given permission in 1900 by the Federal Government to trade breech-
loading rifles at certain stores, including the one at St. Michael
(Oswalt, 1963 b, p. 111). No Kuskokwim station is listed as eligible,
but breech-loading rifles probably were obtained by the Kuskokwim
Eskimos. It appears that throughout the period of occupancy at
Crow Village, guns of all types were rare and difficult to acquire. It
is likely that none of the gun-related objects in the collection belong
to the Russian period. Muzzle-loading firearms probably were intro-

duced early in the American period and continued to be used during
the latter part of the occupancy of the site. Breech-loading rifles in
numbers presumably made their appearance about the time the site
was abandoned.

One possible source of trade goods for Kuskokwim Eskimos was from
the prospectors and miners who searched for mineral wealth along the
river, but before 1898 there were apparently few such individuals.
George C. King prospected for cinnabar around Kolmakov in 1881;
George G. Langtray prospected for gold along the river in 1884; three
unnamed prospectors were in the vicinity of Kolmakov in 1887–88;
and the Frank Densmore party prospected along the Kuskokwim in
1889 (Oswalt, 1963 b, pp. 41–43). The record of known individuals
searching for minerals indicates that they were few in number and
probably had comparatively little to offer the Eskimos in the way of
trade goods. They are mentioned simply to point out the rarity of
Eskimo contacts with outsiders up to the period just before the end of
the last century.

After the purchase of Alaska, the Kuskokwim converts to the Russian Orthodox Church had little contact with their priests. In a report
dated 1878, an Orthodox priest, Father Innokenty K. Shajashnikov,
surveyed conditions along the Bering Sea coast and the Kuskokwim
River. His findings were not encouraging; the church buildings were
in disrepair and remnants of Christianity hardly existed. In 1891,
however, Orthodox missionaries constructed a chapel at Little Russian
Mission. They were responding to Moravian Church activity along
the lower Kuskokwim River following the establishment of the
Moravian mission center at Bethel in 1885. The Orthodox had good
reason for concern since the Moravians opened a second mission station
at Ogavik in 1891. Furthermore, the Roman Catholics founded a mission at nearby Ohagamiut in 1895–96, but it was destroyed by fire in
1903 and abandoned in 1907 (Oswalt, 1963 b, pp. 38, 40, 48). None
of these missionary activities played a major part in the lives of the
Crow Village people. Their contacts with missionaries of any de-
nomination were slight, and no chapel or church was ever built on the
site.

The population of Crow Village and the immediately surrounding
area, embracing a 30 km. radius, was 271 in 1843–44. At the time of
the first American census for southwestern Alaska in 1880, the
downstream village of Ohagamiut had 130 persons; Kalskag, 106;
and Crow Village, 59. Across the river from the later settlement of
Little Russian Mission was Kokhlokhtokhpagamiut with 51 persons
as the only upstream settlement within the radius; this makes a total
of 346 (Petroff, 1884, p. 16). In the Federal census of 1890 we find
Crow Village with 17; Ohagamiut, 36; Kalskag, 29; and Kokhlokhtokh-

pagamiut, 20, for a total of 102. There is good reason to question the validity of the latter enumeration, for there were no major epidemics during this decade. We suspect that this census does not accurately reflect the population of the area. Our suspicion can partially be validated from Weinland's 1884 diary entry for July 7th (Weinland Collection), in which he noted that Kalskag and Ohagamiut each had about 80 residents. Weinland does not record the population of any other villages within the range of our interest. Unfortunately the Federal census of 1900 is so incomplete that it does not aid in reconstructing the population for that period. However, we would be inclined to consider that the figure of nearly 350 for the 1880 census, or a slight increase in this figure, would represent the population number just prior to 1900.

The most critical dates in the history of Crow Village were 1900–1901. During this time an epidemic of influenza accompanied by measles, pneumonia, and whooping cough swept through the Kuskokwim River settlements. A Moravian Church medical missionary, Dr. Joseph H. Romig, recorded the effects of these diseases. Romig estimated that about half of the population died, including all of the babies (Anderson, 1940, pp. 190–205; Romig, 1901, pp. 33–34). This disaster spelled the end of an old way of life, for villages were deserted and the population decimated. About 10 years later John H. Kilbuck (1913, p. 22) made a trip from Akiak to Sleetmiut and remarked, "The population now consists of the younger generation—like the second growth of timber—with here and there a middle-aged person." He notes further, "Villages that were once populous are now either wholly abandoned or inhabited by 25 or 30 persons at most." The abandonment of Crow Village is directly attributable to the epidemic of 1900–1901, and was possibly influenced by the changing river channel which made it difficult to gain access to the village. The traditional culture died largely because there were few remaining people rather than because it was slowly eroded by Whites.

In conclusion it can be noted that an attempt has been made to differentiate between imported manufactured goods from Russian and from American sources. It has been possible to show, largely on the basis of Zagoskin, that a small number of artifacts can, with some degree of certainty, be assigned to the Russian period. At the same time, it has been implicitly, if not explicitly, stated that the extent of Russian influence on the people of Crow Village certainly cannot be estimated on the basis of the artifact assemblage alone. It should be remembered that Russian influence had begun to penetrate the middle Kuskokwim before the establishment of the trading posts and probably even before the establishment of such important coastal stations as Alexandrov and St. Michael redoubts. At the same time,

no evidence has been offered that would refute the general thesis that
the bulk of the Crow Village trade goods is American in origin and
presumably dates from no earlier than 1870 to the abandonment of
the site in the early 20th century.

## LIFE AT CROW VILLAGE: A RECONSTRUCTION

As a result of the excavations, nearly 1,600 items of material culture
were recovered, and from this collection a broad sample of the technology was obtained. The settlement pattern was established by
digging the houses and middens as well as by observing the *kashgee*
cache, and storage pit remains. Archeology could offer comparatively
little additional information about the past of the site. From historical sources we have assembled references to the relationship of the
people with the Russians and Americans, while Eskimos familiar with
Crow Village when it was occupied provided ethnographic fragments.
Although the total data about the site from all of these sources is not
impressive, it is possible to integrate this information and derive a
reasonably accurate view of village culture for the period from the
1840's to about 1900. Drawing additionally on the ethnographic
material collected by Oswalt for the central Kuskokwim River area
from Aniak to Ohagamiut, the picture becomes more complete. In
the reconstruction which follows, when reference is made to excavated
artifacts from Crow Village, detailed descriptions will not be offered
since this information may be obtained from the preceding text. Each
material trait discussed in this section is listed by source in Appendix
table 3. This list includes all the known material objects, where
identification is reasonably certain, for the central Kuskokwim Yupik
during the early historical period. Most of the descriptions are not
drawn with precision because of the nature of the information
available.

Slightly more than 130 years ago when the vicinity of Crow Village,
and probably the village itself, was occupied by Eskimos pushing
inland from the coast, and perhaps across the portage from the Yukon
River as well, the local geography was in its essence the same as it
is today. There were more trees, especially around inhabited areas,
and the river channel was in places building where it is now cutting,
but these geographical changes are not of great significance. At the
same time the faunal picture was different. Beaver were numerous
and marten plentiful, but more important, caribou were abundant.
Caribou frequented the surrounding mountains as the only large
animal of local economic significance. The moose, even by 1900,
was to be found only in the vicinity of Sleetmiut and farther up the
river. Rarely, a hair or bearded seal ascended to the central Kuskokwim from the coast.

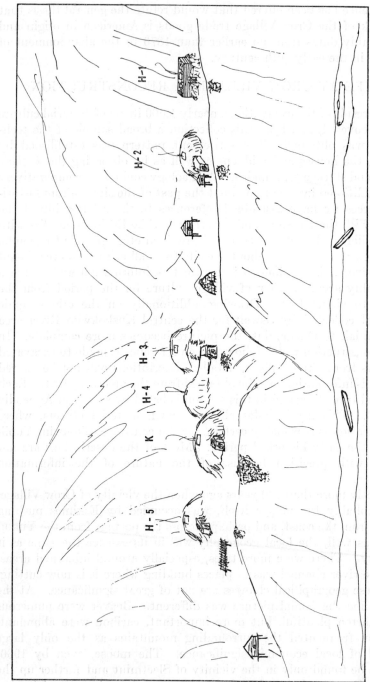

FIGURE 7.—A reconstruction of Crow Village, Alaska.

A summer visitor to Crow Village in the latter part of the 19th century would step ashore on a narrow beach of alluvium. Beyond the water's edge are horsetail, grasses, and a growth of willows reaching to the base of the ridge where pebbles are mixed into the soil. Different types of boats are drawn up on the landing and on the bank behind. There are birchbark canoes decked over for a short distance fore and aft and built around stringers and ribs of birchwood. There are a few sealskin-covered kayaks with large manholes, a mooring hole in the bow, and a projecting stern piece; this type, common farther down the river and along the adjacent sea coast, is rare here. An umiak, or *bidarra* as they are termed locally, is resting upside down on a series of raised logs. Near the *bidarra* and canoes are single bladed sprucewood paddles. Near a kayak is a double bladed paddle also made from spruce but with a ridge running down only one side of the blade. Furthermore, with each kayak and canoe is a set of short spruce poles used to propel these vessels in shallow water.

Along the beach and on the grassy ridge behind the village, persons of both sexes are engaged in the routine activities of daily life. No single type of clothing is worn, but a wide variety of garment forms are to be seen. The men wear trousers of land otter or caribou skin with the fur or hair side out, and beneath these are short underpants of caribou skin. The outer trousers are held up at the waist with a thong, and they reach to just below the knees, where they fit snugly. Suspenders and bibbed overalls are obtained from the traders. Additionally, leggings of caribou skin may be worn by travelers. The parkas of some men are of the winter type with the fur of squirrel, marmot, or caribou hair turned out. These garments are without hoods and reach to just below the knees. They are trimmed in white hair from the sides of a bull caribou's chest, while a wolverine tail dangles from the center of the back of the parka. Bands of white caribou hair encircle the sleeves, and from these are hung strips of otter fur, tufts of red flannel, or tufts of blue or black yarn. Above each cuff of white caribou hair one or more bands of otter or caribou skin are alternated. The opening for the neck is trimmed only in white caribou hair. Other parkas of this type are made of caribou skin but lack the arm trimmings. Some men wear hoodless parkas reaching to their ankles, and from the parkas animal claws and tails dangle. The separate hoods of caribou, marten, or squirrel skins are trimmed with wolf, white caribou hair, or hare, while the inner side of the hood is painted red. The most elaborate hoods have the tail of a wolf or otter dangling from the top. These headpieces are of a form common among the adjacent Athapaskan Indians. Some males wear parkas designed for summer use only; these are of untrimmed caribou fawn skins, reach to the crotch, and may or may not have a hood attached. At least one man wears a broadbrim felt hat on his head. A hooded summer parka designed primarily for rainy weather is made from fishskins or seal intestines and is trimmed with fishskin as well as pieces of skin from land animals. The parkas of the women are of the same general cut as those of the men except that the women's are always hooded, reach to their ankles, and usually are made of squirrel skins. They have long slits up the sides and have more tassels and panels of white caribou hair for decoration. Occasionally a woman is seen with the hood of her parka pushed back and a silk kerchief over her head.

Variation is to be found in the forms of footwear. Socks are made from woven grass, fishskin, or caribou skin with the hair attached. Grass boot liners cushion the feet and are popular for around the village and for short trips. Some men have knee-length boots made from caribou leg skins, with the fur side out, and decorated along the outer and inner lengthwise seams with strips of otter skin from which hang wolverine fur tassels. The bottoms of these boots are made from dehaired bearded sealskins which were obtained by trade from the coastal settlements. Knee-length boots made from fishskins are a popular item for men since they are light and waterproof, but at the same time they wear out quickly and require frequent repairs. Men, but more frequently women, wear boots of sealskin which reach the groin, and the soles again are made from bearded sealskin. Footwear which was obtained from a store includes laced shoes for women, men's shoes, and rubber overshoes. Items of clothing worn only in winter include beaverskin caps for men and mittens or gloves of caribou skin with beaded cuffs. The clothing of the children is simply a diminutive variety of that worn by the adults. Parkas do not have pockets, and therefore each man has a small bag of skin in which he keeps his snuffbox with birchbark sides and a wooden bottom.

People adorn themselves in various ways, particularly around the face and head. Both men and women wear labrets. The lateral lip plugs of men are disk shaped and made from wood or a ground piece of ironstone china worn just below the lateral edges of the lower lip. Men with a medial labret do not wear the lateral variety. Labrets for women are made from ivory and have a hook-shaped outer projection in which there is a hole and from which beads may hang. The ear lobes of the women are pierced, and beads of various colors are suspended from strings which hang from the ear. A woman's nasal septum is pierced, and from a sinew string passed through the hole hang three small blue glass beads. The women also wear necklaces of beads alternated with spent cartridges which have been punctured at the closed end so that a suspension string may be passed through the opening. Likewise, copper bracelets, finger rings of iron or wire, bear-tooth pendants, and pendants of metal are worn. A favored little girl has ornaments on the front of her parka which include beads, as well as large and small brass buttons.

On top of the ridge at the downstream end of the village are a number of holes in the ground. They are as much as 2 m. in depth and are lined with slabs of birchbark. These storage pits are primarily for fresh salmon since they are caught late in the season, are not processed but are placed in the ground to decay. In some of the pits, however, dried fish are placed for winter consumption, and a few storage pits are designed to hold berries. The pits for berries are lined with sewn slabs of birchbark, and into them are set birchbark baskets some 80 cm. in depth and 60 cm. across. Beyond the pits a cache is located in a slight draw. The cache is raised on four posts and built on a log platform. A log framework surmounts the platform. Against it at the front and rear are planks set vertically, while the sidewall planks are horizontal. At the front of the cache is an oval opening, and a low gabled roof covers the structure. Beneath the roof are horizontally arranged poles covered with sheets of birchbark and sprucebark. This covering is held in place by poles along the length of the roof; these are lashed through the bark to the roof poles beneath. The upper poles and covering are bound in place with strips of pliable spruceroot. Leaning against the cache platform is a notched log access ladder, while on the platform is a dogsled stored for later use. The runners of the sleds are usually of spruce although some are made from birchwood. Irrespective of the material, the runners are some 2.5 m. in length, 7 cm. high, and 3 cm. in width. The ends of the runners have an upward bend, and above the stanchions is a flat bed some 76 cm. wide. The sled may be shod with whalebone or wood. Another type of sled, for hauling a canoe or kayak over ice or snow, is also seen. It is about 1.2 m. long with short stanchions and a low bed joined with short crosspieces. Resting on the cache platform are snowshoes made from birch or cottonwood with rawhide thong webbings. The snowshoes are about 1.2 m. long, and they have a turned-up toe. Beneath the cache two to four sled dogs may be tied. Their harnesses, made from old twisted fish nets, are hung from one of the cache poles.

Passing before the cache and climbing up the ridge, the visitor sees a low mound of earth protruding from the hillside. On top of the mound a frame is propped to one side, and over the frame is stretched a thin translucent fishskin covering. Out of the roof opening, which at times is covered by the window, smoke rises from the fireplace below. This, like all the other houses, is occupied by women, girls, and young males. Access to the house entry room is through a low oval opening in a plank wall. In the entry room is a sealskin poke filled with seal oil, and at the opening in the poke is a wooden stopper. A right-angle turn is made to crawl through the tunnel, at the end of which is a step up to the house proper. On either side of the living room is a log extending the length of the structure. These logs separate the walking and fireplace area from the sidewall benches where the residents eat, sleep, work, and lounge. On the benches are layers of grass, and over the grass are animal skins and flannel blankets for bedding. A small saucer-shaped clay lamp from 15 to 20 cm. across rests at the edge of one bed. In the lamp, fish, bear, or seal oil is burned on a wick of compressed moss. In other houses of the village there are lamps raised on wooden stands as well as shallow bowl-shaped lamps of stone or stone lamps with a wide rim and shallow basin. Elsewhere in the community are houses with plank benches, and occasionally stool-shaped supports are placed beneath sagging bench planks. Next to the fire, which is near the center of the floor of any house, are wooden ladles with round or oblong bowls. Beside them is a clay cooking pot which has straight sides and measures some 30 cm. across the bottom; it is not decorated and does not have suspension holes. A situla-shaped vessel with a simple design of lines and dots near the rim also may be seen. The people likewise cook in birchbark baskets by heating stones in the fire and dropping the stones in the basket containing food to be cooked. In spite of the fact that each house has a fireplace, the people have come to accept the use of cast iron stoves.

Although some of the cooking utensils and equipment in the house are from the aboriginal cuture, most have been obtained from the traders. An assortment of tin cans, a few glass bottles, and a drinking glass are scattered about in the house, while a plain metal or enameled teakettle and a frying pan are near the fireplace. Metal pots, a pothook for suspension, buckets, teaspoons, tablespoons, dippers, and ladles, along with an occasional pie tin, are among the trade items. Imported wooden items are rare but include plank boxes and wooden barrels. It is striking that everywhere in the village there is a greater variety of trade goods associated with household activities than with any other segment of the economy. This is all the more apparent when the numerous dishes of metal which have been remade from tin cans are noted. Other containers scattered about the dwelling are made from birchbark. The largest is some 50 cm. square and is used for carrying heavy loads. There are rectangular plates of folded birchbark and a wide assortment of various sized birchbark baskets, dippers, and plates. All of these smaller containers are folded at the corners, and the folds are held in place by bindings of spruce

root or the inner bark of willows.  Some of the more carefully made
vessels have strips of black horsetail root woven into a border design
along the rim.  In order to make certain that the bark from any birch
tree will lend itself to basket or canoe construction a strip of the bark
which includes a lenticel is peeled away from the tree and bent at
right angles to the direction of the lenticel; if the strip does not split,
the bark is considered adequate.  Other vessels are made from
sprucewood planks which have been steamed and bent into an ovoid
shape.  A worked slab of sprucewood forms the bottom, while the
sides are overlapped and bound together with spruce root lashing.
These vessels may be quite small, about 10 cm. across, or up to a meter
across.  Some of these containers have attached wooden handles.
The vessels made by some but not by all men have designs cut into
the bottom to indicate the manufacturer.  Food trays are made from
oblong slabs of spruce and have lips around the edges into which small
ivory inlays are sometimes set.  A burl of spruce is hollowed out
occasionally, and the finished product is used as a dish or storage
bowl.  The same is true for a container made of pecked and then
ground stone.  There are likewise eating dishes made from spruce,
usually ovoid in form.  The cups used are mostly those received from
the traders.  They are either plain or have hand-painted designs or
transfer prints along the sides; unlike cups, imported saucers are
rare.  The family may have an imported pottery teapot.  A few cups
are made from steamed sprucewood with the sides fitted about a
small ovoid wooden bottom; the handle is an extension of the side
beyond the side seam.  A few small containers of woven grass are
found, along with plaited ropes of grass, wads of grass, and small
woven mats, but these are not common in their occurrence. Likewise
there are bags made from fishskins.  In the house also are sprucewood
ladles with very shallow bowls used for serving *agutuk* or fish.

Various sized cutting boards are about the room, and a woman's
ulu with a blade made from tin can metal or ground slate and a
wooden, or less often an antler, handle usually is near at hand.  The
women also have sewing equipment, which includes steel needles, the
back sinew from caribou, bone awls, and numerous pieces of fur for
garments, their trim and repair.  Women are also the ones who make
the fish nets, and their most important netmaking tools are gages for
various sized meshes and shuttles for a ready manipulation of the
netting material.  The netting material is the inner bark stripped
from willow branches in the early spring, twisted grass, rawhide
thongs, or four-ply cotton twine obtained from a trader.  The twine
is separated into a two-ply string in order to extend its use.

Leaving the house, the visitor sees numerous drying racks, from
which fish are hanging, and a dome-shaped structure.  This is a

temporary dwelling erected by the family as their summer residence. It is about 3.5 m. in diameter and is covered with spruce and birch-bark slabs which are tied over a circle of poles stuck into the ground and lashed together at the top. A central opening in the roof allows the smoke from the interior fireplace to drift out. This type of structure may be used for storage, and a similar form covered with grass is sometimes used by travelers who are away from the settlement.

The most striking structure in the settlement is the *kashgee*. This earth-covered mound is higher than any house mound and of greater dimensions. In front of the *kashgee* stands a carved pole with the figure of a bird, probably an eagle, at the top, while at the base of the pole is a life-sized carving of a young girl. The pole was erected by the leading man in the community in memory of his daughter who died in her youth; the bird represents the animal familiar of the man who erected the pole. The relief carving of the girl is adorned with a necklace of beads, ear ornaments hang from the ear lobes, and her face is greasy from being "fed." After pushing aside a brown bearskin doorway covering, the visitor passes into the tunnel entry to the *kashgee*. The tunnel is some 2.5 m. in length, and at the inner end is the men's house. It is some 6 m. across, and the hand-hewn vertical wall logs are as much as 1.2 m. across. Along all four walls are two levels of plank benches. The lower bench is nearly a meter in width, and about 1.8 m. above the floor is a second bench some 60 cm. wide. The lower bench planks are so wide that they could not have been hewn from any locally grown spruce. In the center of the plank-covered floor is an opening about 1.2 m. square; this is the firepit, which is covered with planks when it is not in use. Light penetrates the *kashgee* through the roof opening above the firepit, but still the room is not well lighted because of the soot-darkened walls and cribbed roof. Artificial light is provided by two large bowl-shaped lamps, each resting on a wooden stand adjacent to the sidewall benches about midway along these walls.

Within the *kashgee* are the men and boys who are residents of this structure. They are lounging, chatting, or working on various artifacts. Of all the tools used by the men none is more important than the crooked knife, which has a small metal blade set into the side of an antler or wooden handle. The men also employ a knife with a metal or stone blade set in the end of a handle, and likewise a bayonet has found its way into the community and probably is used as a knife. Metal-bladed axes are to be found, but the more common woodworking tool is the metal- or stone-bladed adz. The stone adz blades are made from flinty material obtained from up the Aniak River or from ground slate. The stone or metal blades are hafted directly on wooden handles or less commonly set into an

antler head. The adzes serve for splitting or planing wood, and the
handles have a slight curve. A wide variety of whetstones exists,
with various grades of coarseness for sharpening different stone and
metal blades. Large grinding stones for the shaping of stone implements are found. Among the other important woodworking and
wood finishing artifacts are the wooden handled beaver tooth drawknife, engraving tool with wooden handle and small metal blade,
drills with stone or metal bits, and an occasional metal-bladed
paring knife or metal awl. Nails are known but are not commonly
used in the construction of wooden objects. Hinged containers are
known but are rare, and the hinges used in one instance are copper.
Metal spikes of brass or iron serve as chisels or wedges.

A man in the process of manufacturing sculptured wooden figures
to adorn a grave spreads before him various types of paint which are
applied to grave objects and to masks. For red paint a sharp stick
is thrust into a nostril until the blood flows. The blood is mixed
with a white or red ocher which has been ground into powder in a
small stone mortar. Black paint is made from coal which is ground
in a mortar and mixed with water. White paint is produced from
the white rock alone and again mixed with water. Blue is a mixture
of ground white paint and rotten pieces of decayed birchwood found
beneath the ground. For a paintbrush the man uses the tail of a
marmot.

Certain raw materials are saved for future utilization. These
include rolls of unworked birchbark, metal cut from tin cans which
has been rolled or folded, and sheet copper. For the manufacture
of antler objects the men prefer to obtain antler from living animals
in the early spring. It is at this time that the antler is said to be
at its hardest and makes the most durable implements. Among
the antler manufactures, which are cut in rough outline with a metal
saw, are net sinkers, wedges, handles for ulus or crooked knives, and
arrowheads. The arrowheads occur in three varieties. One form
is unilaterally barbed; a second form is bilaterally barbed although
both have wedge-shaped tangs. The final type has a flat lanceolate
blade with an open socket.

Outside of the *kashgee* entrance toward the brow of the hill, men
perform various tasks. One may split a tree trunk with the aid
of antler, metal, or wooden wedges struck with a cottonwood maul,
hammerstone, or imported ax. The wooden wedges are made from
the compression wood of spruce trees and are as much as 15 cm. in
length. Near some of the people working out of doors are small
smudge fires in which smoulders rotten wood or fungus from birch
trees. One man makes an object of soft stone which is cut into shape

with a stone saw, then packed and abraded with hammerstones and grinding stones.

A gill net to be set for salmon is placed in a river eddy. The oblong cottonwood bark or spruce root floats are tied to the upper edge of the net, and the lower edge is weighted with pieces of clamped lead, sections of caribou antler attached by lashing holes drilled in the antler, sections of bone notched at the ends, or notched pebbles. These nets are most often 3 to 6 m. in length and are attached to the shore with a rope of willow inner bark. The opposite end is anchored with a rock attached to another rope of willow inner bark. A net set for salmon may be 90 cm. to 1.8 m. wide, including 10 to 15 meshes. A whitefish set net, on the other hand, is 3 m. long and eight meshes deep, 70 to 90 cm. depending on the mesh size. The salmon nets used in drift netting from a canoe are some 20 m. in length and some 1.5 m. wide. The best place to drift with such a net is away from the riverbanks but near a sandbar where there are no obstructions beneath the water. These nets are paid out at right angles to the current from a round birchbark or wooden container which is placed in front of the fisherman in his canoe. The spruce-wood floats for a salmon drift net are oblong with an attachment hole at one end. They are placed at the end of a line which is as much as 1.8 m. from the net; inflated animal bladders likewise may be used as floats. At the far end of the net, away from the canoe to which it is attached, is a wooden float carved to represent a fish duck. A man setting and tending such a net keeps a wooden club or a bone awl in his canoe to kill the fish he takes. The awl is stuck in the neck of the fish in order to prevent it from thrashing, which would tear the net; this precaution is particularly necessary with king salmon. Not only are gill nets set in the river during the summer, but they are used in lakes, such as Whitefish Lake, where whitefish may be netted throughout the year. Furthermore, whitefish, pike, and a species of cod are taken with gill nets set beneath the ice during the winter months.

From a riverbank, salmon are taken with long-handled dip nets some 1.2 m. in diameter at the mouth. Dip nets also may be used in the main river or in small streams in the spring. Spring is the time that fish, particularly whitefish and pike, ascend these streams from the main river. Individual salmon may be speared with a barbed salmon dart made from a piece of iron, or with a leister, which also is used for other large fish. In the winter, up the Aniak River, trout or pike sometimes are taken with a hook and line. A piece of red flannel is tied to a hook and the line paid out from a short rod. Another short pole is held across the line and raised and lowered in the water to attract the fish. As the bait is struck, the fish is quickly lifted from the water onto the ice.

Fishtraps are probably the most efficient means for taking all species of fish. These are constructed from straight splints of spruce-wood bound at right angles to similar splints lashed into circles of decreasing size. The splints are prepared by splitting sections of straight grained spruce tree trunks with wedges and by removing sections of the appropriate size with the wedge-shaped proximal end of an antler crooked knife handle. The splint circles gradually lessen in diameter from the mouth of the trap to the opposite end where the exterior longitudinal splints are bound together. At the mouth is placed a small funnel of splints leading into the trap. Fishtraps may be as much as 1.5 m. wide at the mouth and 5.5 m. in length. They are set in the main river channel in association with weirs of poles and brush or else in narrow streams leading into the Kuskokwim. All the locally available fish may be taken in traps, but there is a greater use of nets in catching salmon.

The fish caught are prepared for storage or immediate consumption by the women. Salmon and whitefish are sun dried on pole racks after being cleaned and split. They may then be smoked above a small fire of cottonwood and placed in a cache or storage pit for later use. Cod are prepared for immediate consumption by cleaning and then boiling them, or else they are preserved by freezing, to be eaten later in a partially thawed state. The meat from any land animal usually is boiled if it is to be consumed in the village, but it may be roasted by men in a hunting camp. For future consumption it will be dried and stored. Berries which have been boiled with fish eggs are stored in birchbark containers in underground pits for later use. Vegetable products are not used in the diet nearly as much as fish and meat; the most important vegetable food is *agutuk* made from berries, usually salmonberries, mixed with meat or fish, vegetable roots or greens, and oil from any large game animal. Berries may be eaten raw as are mushrooms, while young fireweed and wild rhubarb plants are boiled with fish in a soup.

The importance of hunting is much less than that of fishing, but various hunting methods are utilized in taking different land animals. Snares for hares are made from twisted cords of grass and are set along their trails in the snow. Snare loops for squirrels are made from the central rib of a long feather from a bird's wing. They are set along the animal's runway and are attached to a small tree, with the tree serving as a spring pole. The spring pole snare is likewise used in taking hares and lynx. In the spring, deadfalls are used for bear, mink, and marten. Muskrat, mink, land otter, and marten may be taken in fishtraps set in small streams; these traps are usually set for fish alone but sometimes are set specifically for mink or land otter. The people also employ a trap made of netting which entangles a fox or marten. Otter may be killed with arrows or even taken by hand, but the latter method probably is rare. Beaver are taken with a bow and arrow or clubbed to death when they temporarily leave their lodges during a mild spell in winter. Additionally, beaver may be trapped in rawhide nets set beneath the ice during the early fall. From fall until spring the lodge may be broken into after the exits have been blocked; the animals then are removed with an iron hook. Birds are taken with blunt arrows shot from bows or with a bird spear, and ptarmigan in particular are taken with snares.

Hunting black bears in the late fall when they are in prime condition requires the ability first to locate a den. It is said that when a bear walks near his den, he jumps off the trail, leaving no tracks, to the spot where the den is located. When the den has been found, a pole probe is pushed into a hole to locate the head of the sleeping bear, and it is then killed with a lance or the shot from a gun. The lance is made from a wooden shaft with a ground stone point attached to the end. Another bear-hunting method, used in summer when the animal roams about, is to approach the bear so closely that it will stand up a few feet in front of the hunter. The animal is then lanced through the neck. This is a particularly dangerous method of hunting, especially for brown bears.

Most fishing, along with some hunting and snaring, takes place near the village or at the adjacent streams, lakes, and forested or tundra areas. The most adventurous hunting, however, is away from the village locality. In the fall after the major portion of the winter's supply of salmon has been dried, smoked, and cached, the men prepare for their annual fall hunting trip by canoe or kayak up the Aniak or Kuskokwim Rivers. Some men take sinew-backed bows and arrows as well as lances for their major weapons, while others have .44- or .45-.70-caliber rifles or even muskets. The musket balls are cast from lead in a homemade mold of stone; a whalebone ramrod may be used with the musket. Hunters who ascend the Aniak River are interested primarily in taking caribou and bear, while those who go up the Kuskokwim River to Sleetmiut and beyond hope to kill not only caribou and bear but also moose. The men travel upstream and ascend the tributaries in which they are most likely to find game. They hunt until just before the Kuskokwim River is expected to freeze, and then they assemble their catch at a riverbank and build a wide beamed *bidarra* with a frame of bent poles covered with the fresh skins of newly killed large animals. This improvised but highly efficient vessel carries them and their load back to the village.

The processing of skins is one of the many important duties of the women, and it involves the use of diverse artifact forms. First the inner surface of a fresh hide is scraped with a coarse stone scraper made from a boulder chip, and then the skin is rubbed on the inner surface with the grease or marrow from caribou or moose. One form of scraper has a ground stone or metal blade cut from a tin can hafted in a short wooden handle, but the scrapers made from pieces of flinty material or glass are unhafted. The flaked scraper blades are either end or side scrapers. Caribou skins may be prepared for use by scraping them and then sprinkling the inner surface with a powdery white rock found in the riverbank near Ohagamiut. In order to remove the hair, the skin is soaked in water until it begins to decay, and then the hair is removed easily with a coarse scraper. Fishskins likewise are scraped clean with a sandstone scraper, but they are not rubbed with oil or marrow because of their already oily nature.

Diverse types of toys are used by children, and one game is played by men. Children play with bull roarers made from wood; among these people the buzzing sound that the toy makes has no supernatural implications. Segmented dolls of wood are dressed like people and are played with by little girls. Both girls and women employ story-knives to illustrate their "storyknife tales." A game of darts is played; the darts are made from wood but have metal points. A ball made from twisted grass is used to play a game of keep away, and another competitive sport is to see who can chop a hole in the ice the most rapidly. Contests also are held to determine who can succeed in outdistancing his competitors on snowshoes or jump the farthest on foot. Boys are known to play with wooden tops, and *kowchowak* is a popular game played by the boys in the *kashgee*. The *kowchowak* is cone shaped at one end and extends to a flat rectangle at the opposite end. The game is played by trying to flip the dart into holes of various sizes in the floor of the *kashgee*. Checkers also are played in the *kashgee*; this game, of course, was introduced by Whites. Children may play with small models of artifacts used by adults, such as toy bows, salmon darts, bird darts, pistols, and other weapons plus dishes, buckets, and boats. Small carvings of animals in wood include images of bears, mink, caribou, ermine, a "serpent," and loon. It is not certain, however, that these are toys; they may have ceremonial associations as mask appendages or as carvings for graves. The only gambling game known among adult men is the hand game in which two teams of four men each sit opposite one another in the *kashgee*. Each side attempts to guess in which hand one player of the opposite team holds a marked gaming piece. Behind each group of players two men stand and sing songs, no doubt to confuse the guessers of the opposite side. Additional details of the game are not recorded, but individuals are known to have lost considerable amounts of property in the process of playing it.

Returning to the *kashgee* to consider its functions further, it is obvious that this structure is the hub of village life. For not only do the men and older boys live and work here, but it serves additional purposes. It is here that the men bathe in the late afternoon of almost every day that they are in the village. In order to bathe, the window covering is removed and a large sprucewood fire is built in the firepit. The fire may be lighted from a strike-a-light or with a fire drill propelled with a strap. When the smoke from the fire has cleared from the room and the wood has become reduced to a layer of glowing coals, the men remove their clothing and replace the window cover. Each man then sits with a wad of wood shavings stuffed in his mouth and breathes through this respirator. The men wash themselves with urine and scrub their bodies with grass. After the room begins to cool, they sit outside the *kashgee* until they are dry. Then they dress and return inside to wait for their evening meal to be brought in by the women and girls. This and all other meals are prepared by the women in their houses and served to the men and older boys in the *kashgee*. The women eat with the other females and young males in their respective dwellings.

Village ceremonial life centers in the *kashgee*, but not simply in their own *kashgee*. The proximity of Ohagamiut and the fact that they have a much larger *kashgee* frequently induces the Crow Village people to join those of Ohagamiut to present a major ceremony. The practice of having ceremonies in first one village and then the other is reinforced by a system in which each man has a male partner in the other settlement from the same male line as his father's partner. These partnerships are linked to a system of ceremonial exchanges or "potlatches." It is likely also that a man has sexual intercourse with the wife of his partner.

About the time of the Kuskokwim River freezeup each year the people prepare for their winter ceremonials. The face masks manufactured represent animals such as the bear and fox, or birds such as the raven, while still others are in the form of human faces or spirits. These masks are made from spruce from the trunk of a tree or, more preferably, from spruce roots since the roots are carved more readily and tend not to crack. Some of the masks have small wooden carvings attached to the sides on slender pieces of wood; these carvings represent fish, animals, boats, and wands. Each mask has a special song and dance associated with it, and every year new masks are made, new songs composed, and different dance motions developed. A man may make one type of mask one year and another the next year; there is no rigidity to the form of a man's mask.

At this time of the year when the moon becomes new the women prepare food for the particular festivity which occurs. Two men dressed in old and very tattered clothing parade about the village wearing "funny" masks. They go from house to house begging food, and what they receive is placed in woven grass baskets carried by men who follow the masked performers. After all the houses have been visited, the men return to the *kashgee* with the food and feast on it for 3 nights. This particular ceremony, from its description, appears to be a largely secular activity. Another ceremony has supernatural implications that seem to center about a propitiation of the dead and possibly the magical renewal of game; it also is held at about this time of the year. The ceremony centers about the gathering and burning of wild celery stalks (for details see Oswalt, 1957, p. 31).

The specifics or even the gross patterning of the winter "potlatches" and feasts for the dead are not recorded although each is known to exist. It might be anticipated that these are quite elaborate, considering the dramatic effects achieved in central Kuskokwim Eskimo ceremonies in general. When the *kashgee* is prepared for a ceremony, a grass mat or canvas curtain is hung to separate the audience from the preparing performers. When a skit is to be introduced for the first time, the guests eagerly await the performance. The drummers sit on the upper bench beating their tambourine drums, which consist of a handled wooden frame over which is stretched an animal's intestines or stomach. The men beat the drums very slowly with sticks and sing softly so that the assembled people must strain to hear the words being sung. Then the man whose song is being introduced rushes from the audience to behind the stage curtain, strips to his short underpants, and imitates the sounds of the creature he is going to portray. He then sticks his masked face through an opening in the curtain before entering the performing area. From either side of the *kashgee* a woman comes forward to join him; each woman is dressed in her finest parka and holds finger masks in each hand. Some of the finger masks are trimmed with feathers, while others are edged in long caribou hair. Dancing women may at certain performances wear only rain parkas made from intestines. The women keep time to the drums with motions of their arms. Any particular song is sung three times, with each repetition at a faster tempo, until at last the performers sing, dance, and drum as fast as possible.

When the melting snows of spring introduce the month of April, ceremonial attention turns to the subsistence activities for the coming year. In order to try to predict what the year will hold, a doll ceremony is performed. Special dolls are retrieved from their hiding place, and their clothing is inspected for the scales of the species of fish which will be most plentiful or a bit of fur to indicate which of the fur animals most likely will be taken in the year to come (for details see Oswalt, 1963 b, p. 69). In the spring, too, there is an interest in establishing which salmon will arrive first along the central Kuskokwim. When the first fish jumps following the breakup, a man paddles out in his canoe or kayak and with a small birchbark dipper takes water from the river. The water is brought back to shore and tasted by different individuals. From the taste of the water it is thought that it can be predicted which species of salmon will arrive first, the dogs (chum) or king salmon. The reason for this interest is that different gaged nets are required for these respective species, and the nets to be set first are determined by this procedure. The only suggestion of the presence of Russian Orthodox missionary activities among the people is a single carving in wood that may represent a flower and have associations with Christianity.

In the ceremonial life of the village the children are not forgotten. For example, when potlatches are held, each child, no matter how small he or she may be, is always remembered with a gift from a host. The real introduction of a small child to ceremonial life comes when he or she performs a dance for the first time. The performer stands in the *kashgee* holding the skin of an animal, while one adult sings and another dances for the child. After his "performance" the parents distribute gifts to all the assembled guests from other villages. A ceremony for boys is held in the late summer; this gives recognition to their hunting activities during the year (see Oswalt, 1963 b, p. 138).

Along the hillside above Crow Village the dead are buried in small boxes of hand-hewn planks bound together at the corners with spruce roots. The body of the deceased individual is placed in the coffin on its back with the knees drawn up to the chest and hands crossed over the chest. The clothing of the deceased, except that in which he is buried, is burned unless he or she has lived a long time. In this event various items are given to young children so that they too may live long. Some of an individual's small tools and equipment are placed in the coffin, while other small items are given to relatives and good friends as remembrances. On the outside of the coffin of a male may be painted representations of the most important species the man killed during his life. If the man was a great caribou hunter or fisherman, paintings of caribou or fish appear on his coffin. Paintings or small wooden carvings of the most important species hunted by a man are pegged to a board at the head of the coffin. On this board too is very often a carved representation of a man or woman, the sex being the same as that of the individual interred beneath. A separate wooden representation of the person is pegged on the board; for a woman the head is in partial relief and adorned with beads around the neck and hanging from the ears. A few graves have separate wooden carvings of humans. On these the head and shoulders are represented, and the carvings are placed on poles set in the ground near the grave. On top of the closed coffin or surrounding it, strips of birchbark are arranged so that water may not reach the body. At each corner of the burial box is a post, ranging from 45 cm. to 1.5 m. in height, which holds the box up from the ground. Over the grave boxes or stuck in the ground around them are placed larger items belonging to the deceased. For a man his canoe, sled, bow, arrows, and spears are found; for a male child his toy bow, a small boat model, a ball, or top are left.

## ARCHEOLOGY AND ETHNOGRAPHY: INTERPRETATIONS

The rationale for attempting historical archeology along the banks of the central Kuskokwim River was set forth in the Preface. It was pointed out that the difficulties in reconstructing the ethnographic past with informants proved to be insurmountable, and yet the aim was to compile a culture history of the area. The best approach seemed to be to excavate Crow Village first and then to integrate the site findings with informants' statements and historical sources. Now that the excavation is completed and descriptions of the finds offered, along with informants' interpretations and historical references, the authors are *not* satisfied with the results and recognize major difficulties inherent in this type of archeological study. The primary handicap and disappointment in the Crow Village excavation was the absence of a recognizable division between the Russian and American periods. It had been assumed that Russian levels could be isolated in the lower midden and house floors, but this turned out to be impossible. Direct Russian influence on the Eskimos of Crow Village was not intensive, which in part explains the failure. It is likely that similar conditions will be present at other historic sites in Alaska, except perhaps at trading posts and in southeastern Alaska.

Assuming our judgment—that no boundary exists between the Russian and American debris—to be correct, the question is: Does this particular fact lead to any general implications for archeologists? Initially, we wonder whether short-term exotic influences may be isolated in an archeological context. There were at Crow Village nearly two generations of historically documented contact with the Russians, and we have a partial inventory of trade items carried into the area by the Russians. Not *one* Russian artifact, however, was identified with absolute certainty. This fact becomes significant when it is recalled that all of the houses and middens were excavated. The absence of positive identification may stem, in part, from not knowing more about Russian trading inventories, but at best this is only a partial explanation. Judging from our experience at Crow Village we not only question but challenge the precision of evidence for culture contact in prehistoric contexts where the controls are much less adequate. A possible solution to the problem, at least as it pertains to historical archeology, certainly lies in more detailed understanding of relatively subtle changes in the forms of trade goods. Admittedly the analysis of trade goods from Crow Village is not comprehensive. Our ignorance about the nuances of change in trade artifacts points up an important gap in the literature and the need to develop better techniques for dealing with such items. It is axiomatic that the shorter the period of time involved in site occupancy, and the more rapid the rate of change, the more refined the techniques of archeological analysis must be to deal effectively with the problems of interpreting change. It is a simple truth that before we make detailed statements about the cultural changes in Alaska during the 19th century, it will be necessary to learn more about trade goods. A study of museum collections from the early historic period must be made to enlarge our knowledge of trade categories and to assess the chronological significance of changes in style, form, and function. The analysis of trade goods, however, is not the only stumbling block. The techniques of archeology alone are simply too gross to answer, with any degree of certainty, the questions raised at Crow Village. For example, we would like to know how long goods of Russian origin were used at the site prior to the introduction of American-made artifacts. It would be helpful also to know more about the effect of American and Russian forms on each other as well as on the aboriginal manufactures. We contend that the present techniques of archeological excavation and analysis cannot provide satisfactory answers to these questions but that the combined approach produces a clearer picture than using either method alone.

An illustrative parallel to this situation and to the problem it presents can be found in present-day North American culture. Assume that we have visited an old farm in rural Ontario, one that has been occupied continually for the past 85 years. While walking around the farmyard, we note equipment belonging to various periods of the farm's occupancy. In the barn is a new tractor; behind the barn is an old model tractor. In the driveway is the farmer's new pickup truck, and in a field lie the remains of a model T Ford truck, and an even older wagon. In unused sections of the house and in outbuildings lie various pieces of obsolete farm equipment, a milking stool, butter churn, and so on, while in the barn are a milking machine and other up-to-date farm equipment. In attempting to reconstruct life on the farm during the total period of occupancy, we can, of

course, be sure that the wagon was used before the pickup truck and
the milking stool before the milking machine. We cannot, however,
say anything detailed about the rate of change on our Ontario farm,
nor about the nature of change, unless we talk to the farmer, and
then only if his memory or some other source of information extends
back to the establishment of the farm. Only by talking to the farmer
can we find answers to such questions as which new items of farm
equipment were obtained first, what the factors in the selection process
were, and how long the older items were used before they were replaced. Likewise, it is only from the farmer, or from detailed historical data on changing farm equipment and practices, that we may
determine which equipment persisted unchanged the longest in the
face of innovations and which old ideas were given up most quickly.
It is obviously the farmer who can best speak of the intensity with
which he was exposed to different types of equipment and the various
factors which affected his ability and desire to acquire them.

The similarities between the hypothetical farm and the Crow
Village site are apparent. In both cases we are dealing with a brief
span of time which was one of intensive change. The field techniques
of archeology would not be very useful in reconstructing change on the
Ontario farm, and they are not much more useful at Crow Village.
They serve to uncover the material, but beyond that they answer few
of the questions with which we are concerned. It would appear that
one potential for arriving at more meaningful statements about remains such as have been recovered at Crow Village is by a statistical
analysis of the finds. This has not been attempted since our interpretive poverty was not revealed until after an analysis of the materials
by traditional means. In the near future excavations will be con-
ducted at Kolmakov Redoubt and at Kwigiumpainukamiut, which
are contemporaneous with Crow Village, and these will supply a range
of Russian and Indian materials from the central Kuskokwim River
for one period in time. We are not so pessimistic about the potential
of field archeology that we are unwilling to turn to the shovel before
turning to the computer.

Another dilemma of equally as great moment to archeologists was
overwhelmingly apparent after the Crow Village excavations—it
concerns the absences or infrequent occurrences of objects belonging
to the indigenous culture. The absence of fishbones and the scarcity
of animal bones has been discussed and may be understood in terms
of statements by informants. Additionally, there are the absences of
certain artifact complexes. Informants and Zagoskin clearly emphasize
the importance of fishing as a major subsistence pursuit, so that there
is no reason to doubt the focus on fishing. According to these sources,
in early historic times various forms of nets and fishtraps were the

most important devices employed. Among the artifacts from Crow Village were items associated with fishing but not in the frequencies which were anticipated. Only one artifact of inorganic material, a stone net sinker, was found, while netting objects of organic materials included a piece of twisted grass net, numerous wooden and bark net floats, a shuttle, and gages. Considering the extensive nature of the excavation and the excellent conditions for preservation, we expected to find more evidence of netting. If we had had only the artifacts upon which to rely in our total reconstruction, we would have remarked that the people were adjusted poorly to their riverine environment since they did not fish intensively. We were saved from grossly underestimating the importance of netting only by informants and historical records. Another instance of the same nature at Crow Village was the complete absence of evidence for fishtraps, and yet we know that traps were extremely important in the fishing activities of the people. The traps probably were set away from the village, and an old trap would not be brought back to the site. We might, however, have expected evidence for their manufacture. To carry this interpretive problem a step further, we might consider what the situation would have been for Crow Village if we had recovered only artifacts of an inorganic nature. The netting complex would have been represented by a single stone net sinker. In this instance surely we would have stated that netting was very unimportant, or more likely questioned whether this particular artifact really was a net sinker. Archeologists are, of course, aware of this interpretive problem, and it is only by turning to ethnographic analogy and by knowing the environmental setting intimately that broadly drawn conclusions are possible.

The factors of scarcity and absence could and would be offset partially by the excavation of additional sites in the same area and at the same time period. However, if another village site similar to Crow Village were excavated, we would rather expect much the same range of material in the proportions found there. This would not be likely to add greater interpretive dimensions. Temporary campsites, assuming these could be located, might contain a different configuration of artifacts and offer a better balanced view of the culture. Another method of providing a broader perspective of a site such as Crow Village would be by the use of more rigid ethnographic controls. An analysis of riverine ecologies and assemblages around the world, those at the same level of sociocultural complexity, would be a great aid in the interpretation of these archeological remains. It might well be that the conclusions which would be drawn from such an analysis would provide essentially the same kinds of information that are derived intuitively at present. However, con-

firmation of intuition or the rejection of it would be a step toward
a more rigorous methodology and hopefully toward more valid
interpretations.

One of the most frequent concluding remarks in any site report is
that more work is necessary. The archeologist is aware of the severe
limitations of his methodology, and often he attempts to validate
conclusions by multiplying the examples. By contrast most ethnog-
raphers are not so much troubled by incomplete fieldwork. The
typical ethnographer enters the field with a general focal point of
interest or a particular series of postulates he plans to test. It
seems, judging from most ethnographic monographs, that the ethnographer rarely fails in his task, and if shortcomings in his fieldwork
do exist, they are not easily observable. The ethnographer succeeds
where the archeologist fails, because the ethnographer stresses his
strengths and ignores or glosses over his conflicts and omissions. An
artifact on a laboratory table cannot be forgotten as easily as a
dubious ethnographic fact. Quantitative ethnography today does
not suffer as obviously from this failing, but neither is it yet an
important field approach.

In retrospect it is unfortunate that when collecting ethnographic
information in the central Kuskokwim region Oswalt did not seek certain specifics concerning the time of contact. The sessions with informants were structured in a manner which brought forth responses
of a traditional ethnographic nature. It was necessary and desirable
to obtain this kind of information, but another dimension was not ex-
plored. There was no systematic questioning about the specifics of
material changes stemming from the contact situtation, changes which
in all likelihood could have been recalled more readily than facts concerning the aboriginal past. It would have been valuable to learn
which trade goods were preferred, what forms of tin cans first were
obtained, what the cans contained, and so on. Having the specifics
of recent material changes at hand would have made the interpretations of the Crow Village data much simpler, particularly since inventories of trade goods sent to the Kuskokwim during the American
period from 1867 to about 1900 no longer exist.

In the preceding descriptions and discussions, detailed comparisons
with other Eskimo sites have been avoided. The reason for this approach stems from the scarcity of comparative archeological material.
It is important, however, to discuss the only other systematic riverine
archeology among Eskimos of Alaska, the Kobuk River excavations
by James L. Giddings.

During the 1940's a series of sites along the Kobuk River and on
adjacent Kotzebue Sound in northwestern Alaska were located and
excavated. These excavations provide greater continuity between

the prehistoric past and the late prehistoric period than is recorded anywhere else in the American Arctic, with the sites ranging in time from A.D. 1250 to 1760. On the basis of these recoveries Giddings formulated and described the Arctic Woodland Culture. According to Giddings (1952, p. 115), this cultural manifestation, which includes the present Eskimoan-speaking population of the Kobuk River drainage, is characterized:

> . . . by a remarkable adaptation to an environment which includes clear streams, rugged mountains, forests, and a bay of the sea. It is a culture that draws freely upon all of the natural resources of these surroundings, and yet retains a core of basic traits in which may be demonstrated more than 700 years of continuity and stability. River fishing is hardly second to caribou hunting as a means of livelihood, and both of these stand well ahead of harbor sealing as bases of economy. Exchange of the resources of these endeavors as well as materials such as the furs, tree barks and root fibers, and mineral substances, helps to minimize the special effects of local environment and makes possible the enrichment of the life of the individual without his having to move continually from one environment to another.

Giddings further points out that because of unusual environmental relationships, the Arctic Woodland Culture can exist only where forests approach the sea. Neither inland nor coastal adaptations and specializations are required because of the variety of subsistence patterns available to the inhabitants of the Kokuk River drainage. Food products both of the coast and the interior protect the Eskimos against extreme seasonal scarcity and give their way of life a stability that is unknown among more typically interior peoples like the Northern Athapaskans (ibid., pp. 115–116).

Giddings (1952, p. 118) has stated that the Arctic Woodland Culture is a response to a particular set of environmental conditions, the river-forest-sea combination, and should appear wherever these conditions exist. In interpreting this idea, Margaret Lantis (1954, p. 54) regards Giddings' hypothesis as crude environmental determinism and rejects it. To apply the Arctic Woodland Culture concept to a discussion of the Kuskokwim River system where the forest does not reach the sea is to acknowledge that the concept could not fit in its entirety. At the same time there are certain notable characteristics common to the Kobuk and the Kuskokwim River systems. Both are western Alaskan rivers occupied by Eskimos who live in a boreal setting. The Crow Village and Kobuk River sites partially share a diversity in economies with an emphasis on fishing; they both had ties with the coast; and each of these Eskimo peoples had contact with Athapaskan Indians. The most important differences were that the Kobuk people may have placed more emphasis on caribou hunting and probably maintained closer ties with coastal Eskimos, while the Crow

Village people no doubt had closer ties with the Indians and greater economic stability because of the abundance of salmon.

The 11 diagnostic trait complexes and activities employed by Giddings (1952, p. 116) in defining the Arctic Woodland Culture are summarized and listed in table 3. Added to the list are the traits mentioned in the Kobuk River ethnography compiled by Giddings (1961), and the presence or absence of these characteristics on the central Kuskokwim as represented by the Crow Village finds and informants' statements. It is necessary to comment on the nature of the combination of characteristics which have been used to define the Arctic Woodland Culture. Of the 46 characteristics we may eliminate 1 (the underground cache) which occurs twice in the listing and deal only with 45. Since these categories are not at the same conceptual levels, comparisons are difficult. For example, Giddings considered that the extensive use of birch, spruce, and willow as utensils and implements was important, but such a category offers little for comparison. Furthermore, archeological evidence for birchbark or sprucebark canoes, as well as stone boiling in baskets and roasting, is not likely to form useful comparative categories, but then neither were they derived from archeology. Likewise skillful flintworking has an amorphous quality, while the use of a jadeite clearly is of restricted value because of its geographical limitation to the Kobuk. The hard-fired pottery category with textile impressions on the inside and with curvilinear impressions on the outside of a vessel does not occur throughout the series of Kobuk River sites. By eliminating uncomparable categories, localized ones, and a seemingly redundant category, the list is much reduced and the Arctic Woodland Culture loses some of its comparative value.

A comparison of Arctic Woodland Culture characteristics with the Crow Village finds reveals 20 shared characteristics, to which may be added 4 others on the basis of informants' statements. Thus about half are found on the central Kuskokwim in early historic times. On the basis of this comparison the central Kuskokwim Eskimos would not be considered as belonging to the Arctic Woodland Culture in spite of the fact that they occupy the general setting for which this culture was defined. The biggest difference would seem to be that the Kuskokwim people did not have the intensity of coastal contacts found on the Kobuk. However, in Giddings' Kobuk ethnography he states that these contacts were largely in the nature of trade (Giddings, 1961, pp. 9, 128, 139, 147).

Margaret Lantis (1954, p. 55) in one of the most perceptive studies of Eskimo ecology ever written makes a specific comment about the Kobuk and Kuskokwim Eskimos.

TABLE 3.—*Arctic Woodland Culture features compared with the Kobuk Eskimo and central Kuskokwim Eskimo ethnography*

| Arctic Woodland Culture | Kobuk ethnography | Kuskokwim ethnography | |
|---|---|---|---|
| | | Crow Village | Informants |
| 1. Four-post center house | X | X | |
| Central firepit | X | X | |
| Entrance passage | X | X | |
| Underground cache | X | X | |
| 2. Extensive use of antler | | | |
| 3. Fish as principal food | X | X | |
| Fiber net | X | X | |
| Stone sinker | X | X | |
| Antler sinker | X | X | |
| Leister | X | X | |
| Three prong fish spear | X | X | |
| Fish arrow | X | X | |
| Straight shank hook | | | |
| Fish shaped hook | X | | |
| Fish shaped lure | X | | X |
| Gorge | | | X |
| Ice pick | X | | |
| 4. Extensive use of spruce | | X | |
| Extensive use of birch | X | X | |
| Extensive use of willow | X | | |
| Basket | X | X | |
| Barkworking | X | X | |
| Netting | X | X | |
| Root line | X | | X |
| Utensils | ? | ? | |
| Implements | ? | ? | |
| 5. Birchbark boat | X | | X |
| Sprucebark boat | X | | |
| Birch frame snowshoe | | X | |
| 6. Stone boiling in baskets | X | | |
| Roasting foods | X | | X |
| 7. Beaver tooth knife | X | X | |
| Stone pick | | | |
| Soft stone ax | | | |
| Splitting adz | X | X | |
| 8. Skillful flintworking | | | |
| 9. Skinworking method | | | |
| Tci-tho | | X | |
| Powdered white limestone | | ? | |
| 10. Pottery, hard fired | | | |
| Textile impressed outside | | | |
| Curvilinear impressed outside | | | |
| 11. Use of jadeite | X | | |
| Stone saw | | X | |
| Center-hump grindstone | | | |

Returning to the Kobuk for an example: In the fact that Eskimos spending most or all of the year up the river used birchbark and lived chiefly on fish, there is nothing remarkable. Other Eskimos with the same house design, kayak, umiak, bird-spears, fish-spears, etc. who lived along the lower Kuskokwim River used grass, willows, and driftwood (instead of birchbark) and lived principally on fish; and there is nothing remarkable in that, either. The noteworthy trait of both groups is their adaptability while managing to preserve the basic forms of their Eskimo culture. One cannot say that any ethnic group coming into the area will behave the same.

In addition, the following remarks are offered about the attempts to define Eskimo culture (Lantis, 1954, p. 55).

Eskimo culture produces a paradox. Nearly every student of it in Alaska has classified and explained Eskimo culture in terms of one element or one small complex. Collins emphasized harpoon-heads for sea-mammal hunting. Larsen and Rainey emphasized flint-chipping and inland hunting. Now Giddings emphasizes fishing and use of birch, spruce, and willow. Yet the traits that characterize Eskimos and their culture, as William Laughlin has pointed out recently in an astute article, are their versatility, individuation of gear, experimentation, and resulting wide range of variation.

Taking caution from Lantis and questioning the usefulness of the Arctic Woodland Culture as a configuration, we are unwilling to set forth a "culture" based on the experience gained from the Kuskokwim study. Still, riverine Eskimo cultures at the time of historic contact were in many ways distinct from their coastal neighbors. We recognize and stress continuities with the coast but cannot ignore what seem to be significant differences. Perhaps it might be useful to conceive of a configuration of Alaskan riverine Eskimo characteristics. The traits would include diverse fishing techniques for taking salmon and whitefish in particular. We would stress the species taken rather than the particular devices for catching them. The use of trees, whether birch, spruce, cottonwood, alders, or willows, is important, but the specific variations in the wooden manufactures are not. (Perhaps this was Giddings' point for his categories of implements and utensils.) The relative stability of physical settlement is a function of the productivity of the environment and clearly a characteristic of note. There is also the trade with coastal Eskimos in which there is the exchange of forest-riverine products for those of the seacoast. The sociocultural impact of the Athapaskan Indians may not be ignored nor should it be minimized. It should be stressed also that like most Eskimos these people maintained a flexibility in their subsistence pursuits. They exploited land mammals as well as fish, but their economic stability came from fishing.

## LITERATURE CITED

ACKERMAN, R. E.
    1965. Archaeological survey. Glacier Bay National Monument, southeastern Alaska, Pt. II. Washington State Univ., Lab. Anthrop., Rep. Inves. No. 36. Pullman.
ANDERSON, EVA G.
    1940. Dog-team doctor; the story of Dr. Romig. Caldwell, Idaho

BAKER, MARCUS.
    1906. Geographic dictionary of Alaska.  U.S. Geol. Surv. Bull. 299.  [1st ed.,
        Bull. 187, 1902.]
BARBER, E. A.
    1893. The pottery and porcelain of the United States.  London.
BARSUKOV, I., EDITOR.
    1886-88. Tvoreniîâ Innoekentiîâ, Mitropolita Moskovskago.  [3 vols. in 2.]
        Moscow.
    1897-1901. Pisma Innokentiîâ Mitropolita Moskovskago kolomenskago
        1828-1878.  3 vols.  St. Petersburg.
BELANGER, H. N.
    1963. This firm has "spiced" Seattle scene since 1888.  In "Seattle Times
        Sunday Pictorial Magazine," September 22, 1963.
BEMROSE, GEOFFREY.
    1952. Nineteenth century English pottery and porcelain.  London.
BLACKER, J. F.
    n.d. The A B C of English ceramic art (nineteenth century).  Toronto.
BOWMAN, HANK W.
    1958. Famous guns from the Winchester collection.  Greenwich, Conn.
COX, WARREN E.
    1946. The book of pottery and porcelain.  2 vols.  New York.
DE LAGUNA, See LAGUNA, FREDERICA DE.
DOCUMENTS RELATIVE TO THE HISTORY OF ALASKA.
    ———. Alaska history research project, 1936-38.  Univ. Alaska Library
        and the Library of Congress.
DUFFIELD, L. F., and JELKS, E. B.
    1961. The Pearson site.  Univ. Texas, Dept. Anthrop., Archaeol. Ser. No. 4.
FONTANA, BERNARD L.; GREENLEAF, J. CAMERON; ET AL.
    1962. Johnny Ward's ranch.  The Kiva, vol. 28, Nos. 1-2.
GIDDINGS, J. L.
    1952. The Arctic Woodland culture of the Kobuk River.  Univ. Pennsyl-
        vania, Mus. Monogr.
    1961. Kobuk River people.  Univ. Alaska, Stud. Northern Peoples, No. 1.
HAMMERICH, LOUIS L.
    1958. The western Eskimo dialects.  Proc. 32d Inter. Cong. Americanists,
        pp. 632-639.
HEIZER, ROBERT F.
    1956. Archaeology of the Uyak site, Kodiak Island, Alaska.  Univ. Cali-
        fornia, Anthrop. Rec., vol. 17, No. 1.  Berkeley, Calif.
HERRICK, R.
    1957. A report on the Ada site, Kent County, Michigan.  Michigan
        Archaeol., vol. 4, No. 1, pp. 1-27.
HOSLEY, EDWARD H.
    1961. The McGrath Ingalik.  Univ. Alaska, Anthrop. Pap., vol. 9, No. 2,
        pp. 93-113.
HOUGH, WALTER.
    1898. The lamp of the Eskimo.  Ann. Rep. U.S. Nat. Mus. for 1896,
        pp. 1025-1057.
HRDLIČKA, ALEŠ.
    1943. Alaska diary.  Lancaster, Pa.
HUNT, C. B.
    1959. Dating of mining camps with tin cans and bottles.  Geo. Times, vol. 3,
        No. 8, pp. 8-10 and 34.

KARR, CHARLES L., and KARR, CARROLL R.
  1951. Remington handguns. [2d edition.] Harrisburg, Pa.
KILBUCK, J. H.
  1913. Report on the work of the Bureau of Education for the natives of
    Alaska, 1911–1912. U.S. Bur. Educ., Bull. 36, pp. 19–22.
LAGUNA, FREDERICA DE.
  1934. The archaeology of Cook Inlet, Alaska. Univ. Pennsylvania Mus.
    Philadelphia.
  1947. The prehistory of northern North America as seen from the Yukon.
    Soc. American Archeol., Mem. No. 3.
  1956. Chugach prehistory: the archaeology of Prince William Sound, Alaska.
    Univ. Washington, Publ. Anthrop., vol. 13.
LAGUNA, FREDERICA DE, ET AL.
  1964. Archeology of the Yakutat Bay area, Alaska. Bur. Amer. Ethnol.
    Bull. 192.
LANTIS, MARGARET.
  1954. Research on human ecology of the American arctic. Arctic Inst.
    North America. [Mimeographed.]
MADDREN, A. G.
  1915. Gold placers of the lower Kuskokwim, with a note on copper in the
    Russian Mountains. U.S. Geol. Surv. Bull. 262, pp. 292–360.
NELSON, EDWARD W.
  1882. A sledge journey in the delta of the Yukon, northern Alaska, Royal
    Geogr. Soc. Proceed., n.s., vol. 6, pp. 660–670.
  1899. The Eskimo about Bering Strait. 18th Ann. Rep. Bur. Amer. Ethnol.
    for 1896–97, pt. 1, pp. 3–518.
ORCHARD, WILLIAM C.
  1929. Beads and beadwork of the American Indians. Mus. Amer. Indian,
    Contr. vol. 11. Heye Foundation. New York.
ORMSBEE, T. H.
  1959. English china and its mark. Great Neck, N.Y.
OSWALT, WENDELL H.
  1952. The archaeology of Hooper Bay Village, Alaska. Univ. Alaska,
    Anthrop. Pap., vol. 1, No. 1, pp. 47–91.
  1953. The saucer-shaped Eskimo lamp. Univ. Alaska, Anthrop. Pap., vol.
    1, No. 2, pp. 15–23.
  1955. Alaskan pottery; a classification and historical reconstruction. Amer.
    Antiq., vol. 21, No. 1, pp. 32–43.
  1957. A Western Eskimo ethnobotany. Univ. Alaska, Anthrop. Pap., vol.
    6, No. 1, pp. 16–36.
  1962. Historical populations in western Alaska and migration theory.
    Univ. Alaska, Anthrop. Pap., vol. 11, No. 1, pp. 1–14.
  1963a. Napaskiak: an Alaskan Eskimo community. Tucson, Ariz.
  1963b. Mission of change in Alaska; Eskimos and Moravians on the Kuskok-
    wim. San Marino, Calif.
  1964. Traditional storyknife tales of Yuk girls. American Philos. Soc.,
    Proceed., vol. 108, No. 4, pp. 310–336.
PETROFF, I.
  1884. Report on the population, industries, and resources of Alaska. *In*
    U.S. Dept. Interior, 10th census (1880), vol. 8. Washington.
PORTER, R. P.
  1893. Report of population and resources of Alaska at the 11th census:
    1890. Washington.

RAINEY, FROELICH G.
  1939. Archaeology in central Alaska. Amer. Mus. Nat. Hist., Anthrop.
        Pap., No. 36, Pt. 4, pp. 351–405.
ROMIG, JOSEPH H.
  1901. The mission in Alaska, extracts from the report of the Bethel Mission,
        June 1, 1901. Soc. United Brethren for Propagating the Gospel
        among the Heathen, Proceed., pp. 33–34.
RUSSELL, C. P.
  1962. Guns on the early frontiers. Univ. California.
SAVAGE, GEORGE.
  1959. Pottery through the ages. London.
SCHWALBE, ANNA B.
  1951. Dayspring on the Kuskokwim; the story of Moravian missions in
        Alaska. Bethlehem, Pa.
SERVEN, JAMES E.
  1960. Colt firearms, 1836–1960. Santa Ana, Calif.
SINGER, CHARLES, EDITOR.
  1958. A history of technology. Oxford.
SMITH, CARLYLE S.
  1960. Cartridges and bullets from Fort Stevenson, North Dakota. In Bur.
        Amer. Ethnol. Bull. 176, Riv. Bas. Surv. Pap. No. 19, appendix
        pp. 232–238.
STANDARD BRANDS, INC.
  n.d. Cream of Tartar . . . the "Royal" legend. [Mimeographed.]
THORN, C. JORDAN.
  1947. Handbook of old pottery & porcelain marks. New York.
TIKHMENEV, PETR A.
  1861–63. Historical review of the organization of the Russian American
        Company and its activities up to the present time. 2 vols.
        St. Petersburg. [The pages cited are from the unpublished
        translation by D. Krenov dated 1939–40; Library of Congress
        MS.]
VANSTONE, JAMES W.
  1955. Exploring the Copper River country. Pacific Northwest Quart.,
        vol. 46, No. 4, pp. 115–123.
  1959. Russian exploration in interior Alaska. Pacific Northwest Quart.,
        vol. 50, No. 2, pp. 37–47.
WEINLAND COLLECTION.
  ———. The William Henry Weinland collection of manuscripts, letters,
        and diaries. Henry E. Huntington Library, San Marino, Calif.
WILLIAMSON, HAROLD F.
  1952. Winchester, the gun that won the West. Washington, D.C.
WOODWARD, A. L.
  1959. Indian trade goods. Oregon Archaeol. Soc., Screenings, vol. 8, No.3.
  1960. Indian trade goods. Oregon Archaeol. Soc., Screenings, vol. 9, No. 3.
ZAGOSKIN, L. A.
  1956. Puteshestviĭa i issledovaniĭa leĭtenanta Lavrentiĭa Zagoskina v russkoĭ
        Amerike v 1842–1844 gg. Moscow.

Chipped and ground stone tools.  *a*, End scraper of sandy schist.  *b*, Unhafted chert end scraper.  *c*, Semifinished end blade.  *d*, Basaltic end scraper.  *e*, Unhafted side scraper. *f*, Arrow point of blue chert.  *g*, Ulu blade blank, possibly cut with stone saw.  *h*, Blue chert end scraper.  *i*, Worked quartz, possibly hafted snub-nosed scraper.  *j*, Basaltic hammerstone.  *k*, Unfinished end blade.  *l*, Whetstone, possibly used as needle sharpener.  *m*, Whetstone.  *n*, Boulder chip scraper.  *o–r*, Whetstones.

Chipped and ground stone tools.  *a*, Planing adz blade.  *b*, Tapered adz blade.  *c*, Tapered end-hafted skin scraper blade.  *d*, Double bladed skin scraper.  *e*, Symmetrically tanged slate ulu blade.  *f*, Irregularly tanged slate ulu blade.  *g*, *h*, Slate end blade fragments. *i*, Ulu blade without tang.  *j*, Basaltic grinding stone.  *k*, Adz blade fragment.  *l*, Ulu blade with rounded proximal end.  *m*, Stone saw.  *n*, Sandstone bullet mold.  *o*, Stone lamp fragment.  *p*, End hafted skin scraper blade.

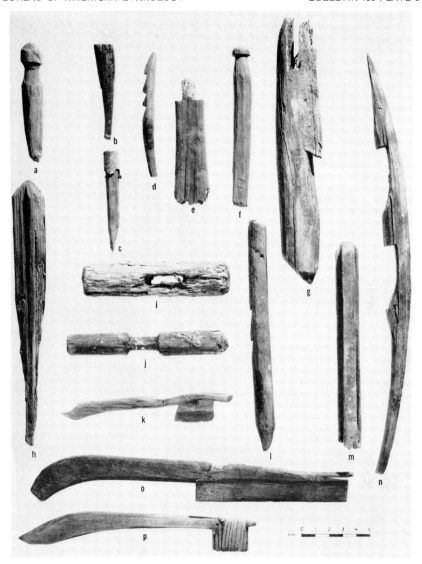

Wooden artifacts.  *a, f,* Snare parts.  *b, h,* Blunt arrowheads.  *c,* Cartridge case blunt arrowhead.  *d, n,* Toy leister prongs.  *e,* Spruce bow fragment.  *g,* Toy lance.  *i, j,* Strap drill handle.  *k, o,* Mesh gage.  *l,* Toy center prong.  *m,* Bird spear fragment. *p,* Mesh gage with spruce root wrapping.

Wooden artifacts. *a, h,* Fire drill shaft. *b,* Cottonwood maul. *c, j,* Scraper handle. *d,* Engraving tool handle. *e ,i,* Ulu handle. *f,* Beaver tooth drawknife handle. *g,* Wedge.

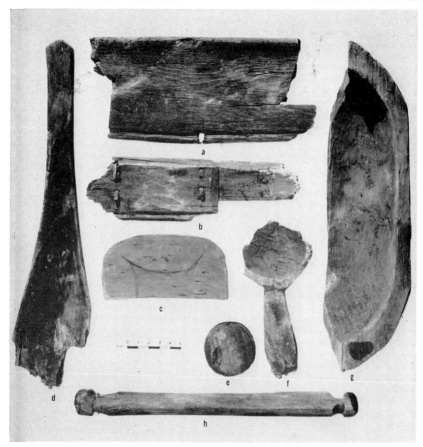

Wooden artifacts. *a*, Vessel side. *b*, Vessel side with root lashings. *c*, Vessel bottom, line-decorated in red paint. *d, f*, Ladles. *e*, Poke stopper. *g*, Sprucewood shallow bowl. *h*, Bucket (?) handle.

Wooden artifacts. *a*, Bark peeler (?). *b*, Cottonwood snowshoe frame section. *c, f*, Section of single bladed paddle. *d*, Medial labret (?). *e*, Carved human face. *g*, Kayak rib. *h*, Wooden peg. *i*, Lateral labret. *j*, Egg-shaped object, toy (?). *k*, Stylized bird, mask appendage (?). *l*, Sprucewood sled stanchion. *m*, Kayak manhole ring side support.

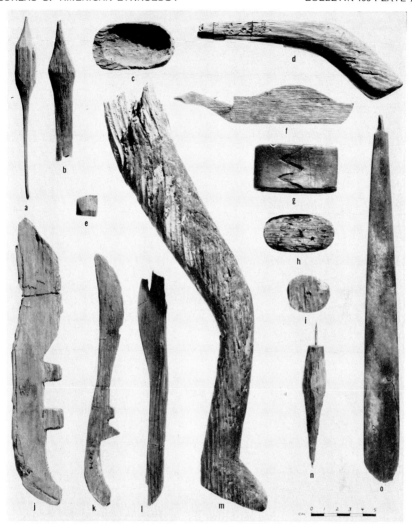

Wooden artifacts. *a*, *b*, Flip darts. *c*, Toy dish. *d*, Toy pistol. *e*, Checker (gaming piece). *f*, Carved bird (loon?). *g*, Wooden snuffbox. *h*, Oblong box lid or bottom. *i*, Portion of snuff, tobacco, or fungus box. *j–l*, Storyknives. *m*, Doll leg. *n*, Target dart with nail insert. *o*, Toy bow.

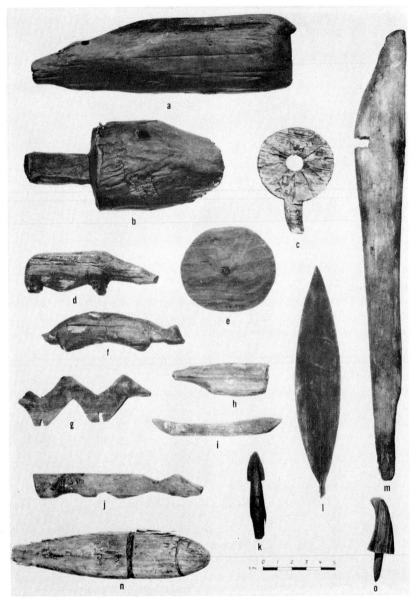

Wooden artifacts. *a*, Carved caribou. *b*, Carved animal head. *c*, Flower carving. *d*, Carved bear. *e*, Wooden spinning top. *f*, Carved mink. *g*, Carved ermine. *h*, Carved caribou. *i*, *l*, Mask appendages, boat model and wand. *j*, Carved "serpent." *k*, Toy salmon dart head. *m*, Drum handle. *n*, Fish carving with suspension groove. *o*, Mask appendage, stylized animal head.

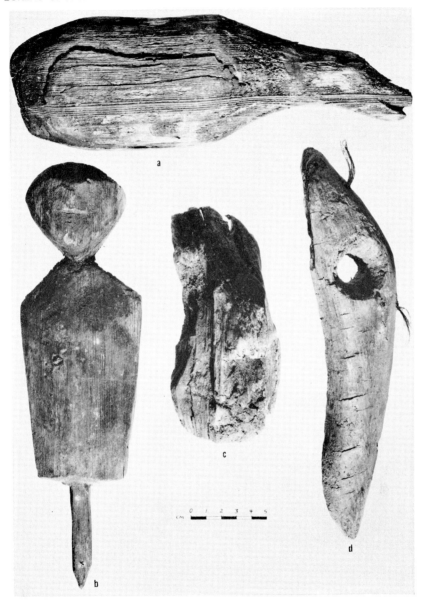

Wooden artifacts.   *a*, Animal carving.   *b*, Carving of human.   *c*, False nose (?).   *d*, Fragment of mask with human hair.

Bone, antler, and ivory artifacts, and locally made pottery. *a*, Bone net sinker. *b*, *d*, Rim sherd, Yukon Line-Dot. *c*, Body sherd, Yukon Line-Dot. *e*, Antler arrowhead (knife blade ?). *f*, Antler side bladed knife handle. *g*, Antler kayak shoe fragment. *h*, Bone awl. *i*, Bone implement (awl, bark peeler ?). *j*, Grooved lamp sherd. *k*, Antler ulu handle. *l*, Antler awl. *m*, Bear tooth pendant. *n*, Lamp fragment. *o*, *p*, Lamp sherds. *q*, Whalebone ramrod fragment.

Bark, wood, and plant fiber artifacts or raw material.  *a, b, c, e,* Birchbark basket fragments.  *d,* Root-lashed wood fragment.  *f,* Plaited grass rope.  *g,* Woven grass section. *h,* Bundle of roots.  *i,* Grass netting.  *j,* Wood handle with spruce root wrapping.

Metal, glass, and pottery artifacts. *a*, Iron salmon dart head. *b*, Skin scraper blade. *c*, Dish. *d*, Pothook. *e*, End bladed knife blade. *f*, Awl. *g*, Glass scraper. *h*, Saw blade. *i*, Scoop (?). *j*, Metal reinforcement piece. *k*, Ferrule. *l*, Leather patches or reinforcement pieces. *m*, Ironstone china labret. *n*, Ulu blade.

Imported pottery and glass bottles. *a*, Transfer print sherd, willow pattern. *b*, Hand-painted ware sherd. *c*, Patent medicine bottle. *d*, Bottle of bluish glass. *e*, Bottle with tapered neck.

Metal artifacts. *a*, Bayonet fragment. *b*, Cast iron planing adz blade. *c*, Cast iron wedge. *d*, Iron spike (used as a chisel ?). *e*, Brass spike used as a chisel. *f*, Teaspoon. *g*, Ax head. *h–j*, Square cut nails—2d, 3d, and 5d pennyweights. *k*, Unidentified. *l*, Kettle lid. *m*, *q*, Buckles. *n*, Copper pendant. *o*, Copper bracelet. *p*, Strike-a-light. *r*, Copper hinge.

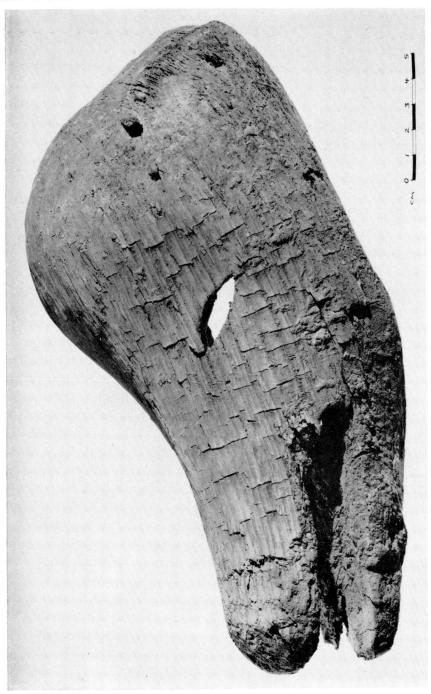

Wooden mask representing a fox.

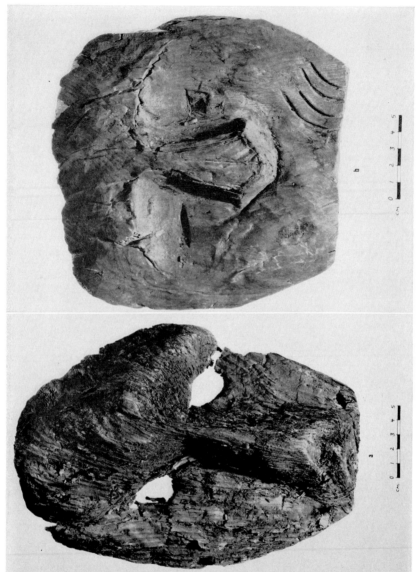

Wooden carvings

*a*, Human mask.                    *b*, Human face.

APPENDIX

APPENDIX TABLE 1.—*Crow Village trait list with locally manufactured items in the sequence of the text descriptions*

| ITEM | LOCATION | | | | | | | |
| --- | --- | --- | --- | --- | --- | --- | --- | --- |
| | House | | | | | Middens and test | | |
| | 1 | 2 | 3 | 4 | 5 | 1 | 2 | 3 |
| Chipped Stone: | | | | | | | | |
| Hammerstone: | | | | | | | | |
| Basalt, flattened at one end____ | ---- | ---- | 1 | ---- | ---- | 4 | ---- | ---- |
| Shaped to fit the hand, used on flat surface____ | 1 | ---- | 1 | 1 | ---- | 1 | ---- | ---- |
| Little chipping except on working surface____ | ---- | ---- | ---- | ---- | ---- | 1 | ---- | ---- |
| Carefully chipped over most surfaces (pl. 1, *j*)____ | ---- | ---- | 1 | ---- | 1 | 1 | ---- | ---- |
| Arrow point, chert (pl. 1, *f*)____ | ---- | ---- | ---- | ---- | ---- | ---- | 1 | ---- |
| End blade blank (pl. 1, *c, k*)____ | ---- | ---- | ---- | 1 | ---- | 4 | ---- | ---- |
| Ulu blade blank, convex cutting edge, no tang (pl. 1, *g*)____ | ---- | ---- | ---- | 2 | ---- | 1 | ---- | ---- |
| Blade or scraper blank____ | ---- | ---- | 2 | 1 | ---- | 9 | ---- | 1 |
| Net sinker, notched basalt pebble__ | ---- | ---- | 1 | ---- | ---- | ---- | ---- | ---- |
| Boulder chip scraper: | | | | | | | | |
| Roughly flaked beach pebble____ | ---- | 1 | 1 | 1 | ---- | ---- | ---- | ---- |
| Flake from large boulder (pl. 1, *n*)____ | ---- | ---- | 1 | ---- | ---- | 3 | ---- | ---- |
| Side scraper: | | | | | | | | |
| Chert, carefully prepared working edge (pl. 1, *e*)____ | ---- | ---- | ---- | ---- | ---- | 1 | ---- | ---- |
| Chert, crude retouched flake____ | ---- | 1 | 4 | ---- | ---- | 2 | ---- | ---- |
| Quartz, steep working edge (pl. 1, *i*)____ | ---- | ---- | 1 | ---- | ---- | 1 | ---- | ---- |
| End scraper blade: | | | | | | | | |
| Chert, steep working edge (pl. 1, *h*)____ | ---- | ---- | 1 | ---- | 1 | ---- | ---- | ---- |
| Basalt (pl. 1, *d*)____ | ---- | ---- | ---- | ---- | ---- | 3 | ---- | ---- |
| Sandy schist (pl. 1, *a*)____ | ---- | ---- | ---- | ---- | ---- | 1 | ---- | ---- |
| Chert, one end shaped as a gouge (pl. 1, *b*)____ | ---- | ---- | ---- | ---- | ---- | 1 | ---- | ---- |
| Chipped fragment____ | ---- | ---- | 1 | 1 | 1 | 5 | ---- | ---- |
| Ground Stone: | | | | | | | | |
| Whetstone: | | | | | | | | |
| Type 1 (pl. 1, *l,m,o*)____ | 2 | 1 | 12 | 18 | 2 | 31 | 4 | ---- |
| " 2 (pl. 1, *p,r*)____ | ---- | ---- | 7 | 4 | ---- | 6 | 2 | ---- |
| " 3 (pl. 1, *q*)____ | ---- | ---- | 3 | 2 | 2 | 5 | ---- | ---- |
| Grinding stone (pl. 2, *j*)____ | ---- | ---- | 1 | ---- | ---- | ---- | ---- | ---- |
| End blade (pl. 2, *g,h*)____ | 2 | ---- | 2 | ---- | 1 | 5 | ---- | ---- |
| Ulu blade: | | | | | | | | |
| Tang symmetrical (pl. 2, *e*)____ | ---- | ---- | ---- | 1 | ---- | ---- | ---- | ---- |
| Tang irregular (pl. 2, *f*)____ | ---- | ---- | 1 | ---- | ---- | ---- | ---- | ---- |
| Tang rounded (pl. 2, *l*)____ | ---- | ---- | ---- | 1 | ---- | ---- | ---- | ---- |
| No tang (pl. 2, *i*)____ | ---- | ---- | ---- | ---- | ---- | 1 | ---- | ---- |
| Fragments____ | ---- | ---- | 6 | 3 | 1 | 7 | ---- | ---- |
| End hafted skin scraper: | | | | | | | | |
| Straight sides (pl. 2, *p*)____ | ---- | ---- | ---- | 1 | ---- | 1 | ---- | ---- |
| Tapered sides (pl. 2, *c*)____ | ---- | ---- | 1 | ---- | ---- | ---- | ---- | ---- |
| Double edge (pl. 2, *d*)____ | ---- | ---- | ---- | 1 | ---- | ---- | ---- | ---- |
| Scraper blade fragment____ | ---- | ---- | ---- | ---- | ---- | 3 | ---- | ---- |

APPENDIX TABLE 1.—*Crow Village trait list with locally manufactured items in the sequence of the text descriptions*—Continued

| ITEM | LOCATION | | | | | | | |
| --- | --- | --- | --- | --- | --- | --- | --- | --- |
| | House | | | | | Middens and test | | |
| | 1 | 2 | 3 | 4 | 5 | 1 | 2 | 3 |
| **Ground Stone—Continued** | | | | | | | | |
| Stone saw fragment (pl. 2, *m*) | | | 3 | | | 1 | | |
| Splitting adz fragment (pl. 2, *k*) | | | | 1 | | 1 | | |
| Planing adz: | | | | | | | | |
| Type 1 (pl. 2, *a*) | | | 1 | 1 | | 2 | | |
| " 2 (pl. 2, *b*) | | | 1 | | | | | |
| Paint mortar | 1 | | | | | | | |
| Stone dish | 1 | | | | | | | |
| Lamp fragment: | | | | | | | | |
| Crudely chipped | | | | | | 1 | | |
| Flat rim, shallow bowl (pl. 2, *o*) | | | | | | 1 | | |
| Bullet mold half (pl. 2, *n*) | | | | 1 | | | | |
| **Wood:** | | | | | | | | |
| Fishing: | | | | | | | | |
| Mesh gage (pl. 3, *k, o, p*) | | | 1 | 1 | | 6 | | |
| Net float | | | | | 1 | 6 | | |
| Net shuttle | | | | 1 | | | | |
| Fishing rod | | | | | 1 | 1 | | |
| Land hunting: | | | | | | | | |
| Blunt arrowhead: | | | | | | | | |
| Multifaceted tip (pl. 3, *h*) | | | | | | | 1 | |
| Flat across the tip (pl. 3, *b*) | | | | | | 1 | | |
| Empty cartridge case over tip (pl. 3, *c*) | | | | | | 1 | | |
| Bow fragment (pl. 3, *e*) | | | | 1 | | 7 | | |
| Bird spear shaft fragment (pl. 3, *m*) | | | | | | 3 | | |
| Snare peg (pl. 3, *a, f*) | | | | | | 4 | | |
| Tools: | | | | | | | | |
| Wedge (pl. 4, *g*) | | | 6 | | 1 | 11 | | |
| Used as fire drill board | | | | | | 1 | | |
| Beaver tooth drawknife handle (pl. 4, *f*) | | | | | | 4 | | |
| Engraving tool handle: | | | | | | | | |
| Notched for blade with lashing lip (pl. 4, *d*) | | | | | | 1 | | |
| Split base and lashing grooves | | | | | | 2 | | |
| Ulu handle: | | | | | | | | |
| Curved blade slit (pl. 4, *e*) | | | | | | 1 | | |
| Straight blade slit, hole for grip (pl. 4, *i*) | | | | | | 1 | | |
| Scraper handle: | | | | | | | | |
| Straight (pl. 4, *c*) | | | | | | 1 | | |
| Curved (pl. 4, *j*) | | | | | | 1 | | |
| Adz handle, cottonwood | | | 1 | 1 | | | | |
| Fire drill shaft (pl. 4, *a*) | | | | | | 4 | | |
| Drill shaft (pl. 4, *h*) | | | | | | 1 | | |
| Drill strap handle: | | | | | | | | |
| Hole in center (pl. 3, *i*) | | | | | | | 1 | |
| Grooved center (pl. 3, *j*) | | | 1 | | | 1 | | |

APPENDIX TABLE 1.—*Crow Village trait list with locally manufactured items in the sequence of the text descriptions*—Continued

| ITEM | House | | | | | Middens and test | | |
|---|---|---|---|---|---|---|---|---|
| | 1 | 2 | 3 | 4 | 5 | 1 | 2 | 3 |
| **Wood—Continued** | | | | | | | | |
| **Tools—Continued** | | | | | | | | |
| Maul: | | | | | | | | |
| Cottonwood (pl. 4, b) | | | 1 | 1 | 1 | | | |
| Paddle shaped | | | | | | 1 | | |
| Stake | 1 | | 1 | 1 | | 2 | 1 | |
| Household equipment: | | | | | | | | |
| Cutting board fragment | | | 2 | 2 | | | | |
| Handle (pl. 5, h) | | | | | | 1 | | |
| Ladle: | | | | | | | | |
| Deep rounded bowl (pl. 5, f) | | | | | | 1 | 1 | |
| Shallow oblong bowl (pl. 5, d) | | | | 1 | 1 | 1 | | |
| Thin handle fragment | | | | | | | 1 | |
| Poke stopper (pl. 5, e) | | | | | | 1 | | |
| Vessel bottom: | | | | | | | | |
| Fragment | | | | | | 1 | 1 | |
| Decorated (pl. 5, c) | | | | | | 1 | | |
| Vessel side: | | | | | | | | |
| Grooved (pl. 5, a) | | | | | | 2 | | |
| Showing lashing (pl. 5, b) | | | | | | 1 | | |
| Thin | | | | | | 2 | | |
| Dish: | | | | | | | | |
| Shallow, wide, flat rim | | 1 | | | | 1 | | |
| Oblong, rimless | | | | 1 | 1 | | | |
| Fragment | | | | | | 3 | | |
| Bowl (pl. 5, g) | | | | | | 1 | | |
| Bench support | | | | 3 | | | | |
| Lampstand | 1 | | | 2 | | | | |
| **Transportation:** | | | | | | | | |
| Kayak: | | | | | | | | |
| Bow fragment | | | | | | 1 | | |
| Manhole ring section | | | | | | 1 | | |
| Side support for manhole ring (pl. 6, m) | | | | | | 1 | | |
| Deck support | | | | | | 1 | | |
| Rib (pl. 6, g) | | | | | | 2 | | |
| Paddle: | | | | | | | | |
| Handle (pl. 6, c) | | | | 1 | | 1 | 1 | |
| Ribbed blade fragment (pl. 6, f) | | | | | | 3 | | |
| Flat blade fragment | | | | | | 1 | | |
| Canoe or kayak sled crosspiece | | | | | | | 1 | |
| Sled: | | | | | | | | |
| Stanchion (pl. 6, l) | | | 1 | | | | | |
| Runner fragment | | | 1 | 1 | | | | |
| Curved end | | | | 1 | | | | |
| Shoe section | | | 1 | 1 | | | | |
| Snowshoe frame section (pl. 6, b) | | | | 1 | | | | |

APPENDIX TABLE 1.—*Crow Village trait list with locally manufactured items in the sequence of the text descriptions*—Continued

| ITEM | House | | | | | Middens and test | | |
|---|---|---|---|---|---|---|---|---|
| | 1 | 2 | 3 | 4 | 5 | 1 | 2 | 3 |
| Wood—Continued | | | | | | | | |
| Personal adornment: | | | | | | | | |
| Labret: | | | | | | | | |
| Lateral (pl. 6, i) | | | | | | 3 | | |
| Medial (pl. 6, d) | | | | | | 1 | | |
| Tobacco complex: | | | | | | | | |
| Snuffbox (pl. 7, g) | | | | | | 1 | | |
| Snuff or tobacco box, lid and bottom: | | | | | | | | |
| Round (pl. 7, i) | | | | | | 6 | 2 | |
| Oval (pl. 7, h) | | | 2 | | | 1 | 2 | |
| Games and toys: | | | | | | | | |
| Top (pl. 8, e) | | | 1 | | | 2 | 1 | |
| Checker (pl. 7, e) | | | | | | 2 | | |
| Flip dart (pl. 7, a, b) | | | 5 | 1 | 1 | 13 | 6 | |
| Dart (pl. 7, m) | | | | 1 | 1 | 1 | 1 | |
| Storyknife: | | | | | | | | |
| Straight handle (pl. 7, l) | | | | | | 1 | 1 | |
| Animal shape (pl. 7, j, k) | | | | | 1 | 1 | | |
| Bow fragment (pl. 7, o) | | | | | 1 | 3 | | |
| Salmon dart head (pl. 8, k) | | | | | | | 1 | |
| Dish (pl. 7, c) | | | 1 | | | | | |
| Bucket bottom | | | | | | 1 | | |
| Boat | | | | | | | 1 | |
| Leister prong fragment (pl. 3, d, n) | | | | | | 4 | | |
| Fish spear center prong fragment (pl. 3, l) | | | | | | 1 | | |
| Lance fragment (pl. 3, g) | | | | | | 1 | | |
| Pistol (pl. 7, d) | | | | | | | 1 | |
| Segmented doll section (pl. 7, m) | | | 4 | | | | | |
| Animal carving: | | | | | | | | |
| Bear (pl. 8, d) | | | 1 | | | | | |
| Mink (pl. 8, f) | | | | | | | 1 | |
| Caribou (pl. 8, h) | | | | | | 1 | | |
| "Serpent" (pl. 8, j) | | | | | | | 1 | |
| Ermine (pl. 8, g) | | | | | | | 1 | |
| Bird carving: | | | | | | | | |
| Loon (pl. 7, f) | | | | | 1 | | | |
| Animal head: | | | | | | | | |
| Caribou, unfinished | | | | | | 1 | | |
| Ceremonial objects: | | | | | | | | |
| Memorial image: | | | | | | | | |
| Caribou carving, slot under body (pl. 9, a) | | | | | | 4 | | |
| Caribou carving, holes for antlers and legs (pl. 8, a) | | | | | | | 1 | |
| Human carving (pl. 9, b) | | | | | | 2 | | |
| Animal head (pl. 8, b) | | | | | | | 1 | |

APPENDIX TABLE 1.—*Crow Village trait list with locally manufactured items in the sequence of the text descriptions*—Continued

| ITEM | House | | | | | Middens and test | | |
|---|---|---|---|---|---|---|---|---|
| | 1 | 2 | 3 | 4 | 5 | 1 | 2 | 3 |
| Wood—Continued | | | | | | | | |
| Ceremonial objects—Continued | | | | | | | | |
| Mask: | | | | | | | | |
| Human face (pl. 16, a) | | | 1 | | | | | |
| Human face, no eyeholes (pl. 16, b) | | | | | | 1 | | |
| Fox (pl. 15) | | | 1 | | | | | |
| Half a human face with human hair (pl. 9, d) | | | 1 | | | | | |
| False human nose (pl. 9, c) | | | 1 | | | | | |
| Fragment | | | | | | 2 | | |
| Mask appendage: | | | | | | | | |
| Wand (pl. 8, l) | | | | | | 2 | | |
| Boat (pl. 8, i) | | | 1 | | | | | |
| Animal or bird head (pl. 8, o) | | | 1 | | | | 1 | |
| Outer ring of mask (?) | | | | | | 1 | | |
| Fish carving (pl. 8, n) | | | 1 | | | 1 | | |
| Drum handle (pl. 8, m) | | | | | | 1 | | |
| Flower (?) carving (pl. 8, c) | 1 | | | | | | | |
| Miscellaneous and Unidentified: | | | | | | | | |
| Peg (pl. 6, h) | | | | | | 3 | | |
| Inserted in wood fragment | | | | | | 2 | | |
| Unidentified objects (pl. 6, a, e, j, k) | | | 3 | 1 | | 2 | 4 | |
| Fragments | | | 8 | 5 | 2 | 93 | 10 | |
| Bone and Antler: | | | | | | | | |
| Net sinker: | | | | | | | | |
| Antler, drilled holes | | 1 | | 1 | | 1 | 1 | |
| Bone, notched (pl. 10, a) | | | | | | 1 | | |
| Ramrod, whalebone (pl. 10, q) | | 1 | | | | | | |
| Arrowhead, antler, open socket (pl. 10, e) | | | | | | | 1 | |
| Wedge, antler | | | 3 | 1 | | 3 | 4 | |
| Awl, bone: | | | | | | | | |
| Type 1 (pl. 10, h) | | | 1 | | | 1 | | |
| Type 2 (pl. 10, l) | | | | 2 | | | | |
| Spatulate shaped at one end (pl. 10, i) | | | 1 | | | | | |
| Ulu handle, antler, decorated (pl. 10, k) | | | | | | | 1 | |
| Side bladed knife handle, antler (pl. 10, f) | | | | 1 | | | | |
| Adz head, antler, unfinished | | | | | | 1 | | |
| Sled shoe, whalebone section | | | | | | 11 | 1 | |
| Bow or stern shoe for kayak, antler (pl. 10, g) | | | | | | 1 | | |
| Bear tooth pendant (pl. 10, m) | | | | | | | 1 | |
| Worked caribou antler fragment | | | | | | 3 | 1 | |
| Clay: | | | | | | | | |
| Pot sherds (pl. 10, b, c, d) | 5 | 1 | 15 | 14 | 1 | 24 | 1 | |
| Lamp sherds, saucer shaped (pl. 10, j, m, n, o) | 1 | | 4 | 2 | | 5 | 3 | |

APPENDIX TABLE 1.—*Crow Village trait list with locally manufactured items in the sequence of the text descriptions*—Continued

| | LOCATION | | | | | | | |
| ITEM | House | | | | | Middens and test | | |
| | 1 | 2 | 3 | 4 | 5 | 1 | 2 | 3 |
|---|---|---|---|---|---|---|---|---|
| **Grass:** | | | | | | | | |
| Bunches | | | | | | 3 | | |
| Plaited rope (pl. 11, f) | | | | | | 1 | 7 | |
| Twisted netting (pl. 11, i) | | | | | | 1 | | |
| Woven (pl. 11, g) | | | 3 | 1 | | | | |
| **Bark and Root:** | | | | | | | | |
| Birchbark: | | | | | | | | |
| Basket | 1 | | 3 | 1 | | 1 | 3 | |
| Fragment (pl. 11, b, c) | 1 | | 1 | 1 | | 4 | | |
| Sewn fragment (pl. 11, a, e) | | | | | | 11 | | |
| Cottonwood bark: | | | | | | | | |
| Net float | | | | 1 | | 10 | | |
| Fragment | | | | 1 | | 18 | | |
| Blank | | | | | | 5 | | |
| Spruce root: | | | | | | | | |
| Wrapped sticks (pl. 11, d) | | | | | | 3 | | |
| Wrapped handle (pl. 11, j) | | | | | | 1 | | |
| Bundle (pl. 11, h) | | | 1 | | | | | |
| **Metal:** | | | | | | | | |
| Salmon dart head (pl. 12, a) | | | 1 | | | | | |
| Musket ball | | | 6 | | | | | |
| Pothook (pl. 12, d) | | | | | | | 1 | |
| End bladed knife blade (pl. 12, e) | | | | | | 1 | | |
| Saw blade fragment (pl. 12, h) | | | | | | 2 | | |
| Awl (pl. 12, f) | | | | | | 1 | | |
| Ulu blade (pl. 12, n) | 2 | | 2 | | | | 1 | |
| Skin scraper blade (pl. 12, b) | | | | 2 | | | | |
| Dish (pl. 12, c, i) | 2 | 2 | | 2 | | | 3 | |
| Reinforcement piece (pl. 12, j) | | | 1 | | 1 | | 2 | |
| Log reinforcement piece (?) | | | | 4 | | | | |
| Cut can fragments | 3 | 3 | 4 | 5 | 1 | 1 | 9 | |
| Bucket handle section | | | | 1 | | | 1 | |
| Cut sheet of copper | | | | 1 | | | | |
| Ferrule (pl. 12, k) | | | | 1 | | | | |
| .22 caliber cartridge drilled as a bead | 4 | | | | | | | |
| Drilled cartridge case with beads attached | | | | | | | 1 | |
| **Glass:** | | | | | | | | |
| Scraper: | | | | | | | | |
| Green bottle fragment | 2 | | 1 | | | | | |
| Brown bottle fragment (pl. 12, g) | | | | 1 | | | | |
| Window glass | | | 1 | | | 1 | | |
| **Non-Eskimo Pottery:** | | | | | | | | |
| Labret, ironstone china (pl. 12, m) | | | | | | 1 | | |
| **Leather:** | | | | | | | | |
| Patch or reinforcement piece (pl. 12, l) | | 2 | | | | 1 | | |

APPENDIX TABLE 2.—*Crow Village trait list with imported manufactured items in the sequence of the text descriptions*

| ITEM | LOCATION | | | | | | | |
| --- | --- | --- | --- | --- | --- | --- | --- | --- |
| | House | | | | | Middens and test | | |
| | 1 | 2 | 3 | 4 | 5 | 1 | 2 | 3 |
| Non-Eskimo pottery: | | | | | | | | |
| Plain white, undecorated fragment | 14 | 20 | 46 | 17 | 7 | 3 | 57 | ---- |
| White cup, undecorated | ---- | ---- | 1 | ---- | ---- | ---- | ---- | ---- |
| Transfer print ware fragment (pl. 13, a) | 4 | 10 | 15 | 4 | 4 | 4 | 8 | 4 |
| Saucer | ---- | ---- | 1 | ---- | ---- | ---- | ---- | ---- |
| Hand painted ware fragment (pl. 13, b) | 8 | 9 | 27 | 4 | 6 | 9 | 34 | 1 |
| Glazed teapot fragment | ---- | ---- | ---- | ---- | ---- | ---- | 3 | ---- |
| Blue painted kitchen ware fragment | ---- | ---- | 3 | ---- | ---- | ---- | ---- | ---- |
| Glass: | | | | | | | | |
| Button, four hole | 1 | ---- | ---- | 2 | ---- | ---- | 2 | ---- |
| Window glass fragment | 12 | 16 | 12 | 3 | ---- | 3 | 13 | ---- |
| Bottle: | | | | | | | | |
| Patent medicine, complete (pl. 13, c) | ---- | ---- | 1 | 1 | ---- | ---- | ---- | ---- |
| Soft drink (?) (pl. 13, e) | ---- | ---- | 1 | ---- | ---- | ---- | ---- | ---- |
| Use unknown (pl. 13, d) | ---- | ---- | 1 | ---- | ---- | ---- | ---- | ---- |
| Fragment | 6 | 1 | 3 | 1 | 2 | ---- | ---- | ---- |
| Drinking glass fragment | 1 | ---- | 1 | 1 | ---- | ---- | ---- | ---- |
| Lamp chimney (?) fragment | 1 | ---- | ---- | ---- | ---- | ---- | 1 | ---- |
| Bead: | | | | | | | | |
| White | 50 | 8 | 22 | 20 | 2 | 110 | 38 | ---- |
| Blue | 24 | 1 | 5 | 4 | 1 | 74 | 8 | ---- |
| White lined red | ---- | 3 | 2 | 2 | ---- | ---- | 1 | ---- |
| Green | ---- | ---- | ---- | ---- | ---- | 3 | ---- | ---- |
| Green lined red | ---- | ---- | 1 | ---- | ---- | 5 | 1 | ---- |
| Black | 14 | ---- | ---- | ---- | ---- | 6 | ---- | ---- |
| Red | 1 | ---- | 1 | 3 | ---- | 1 | 1 | ---- |
| Yellow | ---- | ---- | ---- | 1 | ---- | ---- | 1 | ---- |
| Blue lined white, painted | ---- | ---- | ---- | 1 | ---- | ---- | 1 | ---- |
| Metal: | | | | | | | | |
| Nail: | | | | | | | | |
| Wire | ---- | ---- | ---- | 7 | ---- | ---- | 5+ | 5 |
| Square cut (pl. 14, h–j) | ---- | ---- | 2 | 4 | ---- | ---- | ---- | ---- |
| Tin can: | | | | | | | | |
| Type 1 | ---- | ---- | 1 | ---- | ---- | ---- | ---- | ---- |
| " 2 | ---- | 1 | ---- | ---- | ---- | ---- | ---- | ---- |
| " 3 | 1 | ---- | ---- | ---- | ---- | ---- | ---- | ---- |
| " 4 | 1 | 2 | ---- | ---- | ---- | ---- | ---- | ---- |
| " 5 | 4 | ---- | 2 | ---- | ---- | ---- | ---- | ---- |
| " 6 | 1 | 1 | ---- | ---- | ---- | ---- | ---- | ---- |
| " 7 | ---- | 1 | 1 | 1 | ---- | ---- | ---- | 1 |
| " 8 | ---- | ---- | 1 | ---- | ---- | ---- | ---- | ---- |
| " 9 | ---- | ---- | ---- | ---- | 1 | 1 | 3 | ---- |
| " 10 | 1 | ---- | 1 | ---- | ---- | ---- | 1 | ---- |
| " 11 | ---- | 1 | ---- | ---- | ---- | ---- | ---- | ---- |
| Untyped | 1 | ---- | ---- | 1 | 2 | ---- | ---- | 1 |
| Fragment | 9 | 15 | 9 | 13 | 6 | 4 | 4 | ---- |

APPENDIX TABLE 2.—*Crow Village trait list with imported manufactured items in the sequence of the text descriptions*—Continued

| ITEM | LOCATION | | | | | | | |
| | House | | | | | Middens and test | | |
| | 1 | 2 | 3 | 4 | 5 | 1 | 2 | 3 |
|---|---|---|---|---|---|---|---|---|
| Metal—Continued | | | | | | | | |
| Cartridge: | | | | | | | | |
|   .44-caliber: | | | | | | | | |
|     Rimfire | | | 1 | | | | 1 | |
|     Center-fire, Winchester | 1 | | | | | | | |
|   .45-.70-caliber, center-fire | | | | | | | 1 | |
| Enameled teakettle | 1 | | | | | | | |
| Sheet iron frying pan | 1 | | | | | | | |
| Flat bottomed iron bucket | | | | 1 | | | | |
| Pie tin | | | | | | | | 1 |
| Kettle fragment | | 1 | 2 | | | | | |
| Bucket fragment | | | 5 | | | 1 | | |
| Kettle lid (pl. 14, *l*) | | | | | 2 | | | |
| Spoon: | | | | | | | | |
|   Tea (pl. 14, *f*) | 1 | | | | | | | |
|   Serving | | | | 1 | | | | |
|   Table | | | 1 | | | | | |
| Dipper handle | 1 | | | | | | | |
| Copper hinge (pl. 14, *r*) | | | | 1 | | | | |
| Stove fragment | | | 1 | 1 | 1 | 1 | 1 | |
| Wedge (pl. 14, *c*) | | | | 1 | | | | |
| Planing adz blade (pl. 14, *b*) | 1 | | | | | | | |
| Ax head: | | | | | | | | |
|   Steel | | 1 | | | | | | |
|   Iron, hand forged (pl. 14, *g*) | | | | 1 | | | | |
| Strike-a-light (pl. 14, *p*) | | | | | | | 1 | |
| Chisel: | | | | | | | | |
|   Brass spike (pl. 14, *e*) | | | | 1 | | | | |
|   Iron spike (pl. 14, *d*) | | | | 1 | | | | |
| Suspender buckle (pl. 14, *q*) | | | | | | | | 1 |
| Overall strap buckle (pl. 14, *m*) | | | | | | | 1 | |
| Copper bracelet (pl. 14, *o*) | | | | 1 | | | | |
| Pendant (pl. 14, *n*) | | 1 | | | | | | |
| Iron scrap | 4 | 3 | 2 | 2 | | 5 | 1 | 1 |
| Bayonet section (pl. 14, *a*) | | | 1 | | | | | |
| Iron object, unidentified (pl. 14, *k*) | | | 1 | | | | | |
| Wood: | | | | | | | | |
| Box: | | | | | | | | |
|   Fragment | | | | 1 | | | | |
|   Cigarbox section | | | | | | | 1 | |
| Barrel stave | | | | 1 | | | | |
| Paring knife handle section | | | | | | 1 | 1 | |
| Textiles and Footwear: | | | | | | | | |
| Wide brim hat, felt | | | | 1 | | | | |
| Kerchief, silk | | | | | | | 1 | |
| Textile scraps | | | 3 | | | 1 | | |
| Overshoe, section | | | 1 | | | | | |
| Man's square toe shoe section | 1 | | | | | | | |
| Woman's laced boot | | | 1 | | | | | |
| Miscellaneous: | | | | | | | | |
| Lump of tar | | | | 1 | | | | |

APPENDIX TABLE 3.—*Central Kuskokwim Yuk culture, circa 1840–1900*

| Item | Source |
|---|---|
| Settlement Pattern: | |
| Cache: | |
| Entry, oval hole | Informants. |
| Ladder, notched log | Do. |
| Platform, log | Do. |
| Roof, gabled | Do. |
| Supports, four posts | Crow Village; Informants. |
| Walls, horizontal planks | Informants. |
| Dwelling: | |
| Summer: | |
| Pole frame | Do. |
| Cover: | |
| Birchbark | Do. |
| Grass | Do. |
| Winter: | |
| Log frame (see Figure 6) | Crow Village. |
| Fishskin window | Informants. |
| *Kashgee* | |
| Benches, two rows | Informants; Zagoskin. |
| Entrance, tunnel | Crow Village; Informants. |
| Fire pit, central | Informants. |
| Roof, cribbed | Do. |
| Walls, vertical hewn logs | Crow Village; Informants. |
| Rack for drying fish | Informants. |
| Storage pit; birchbark lined | Crow Village; Informants. |
| Clothing: | |
| European: | |
| Button, glass | Crow Village. |
| Hat; felt, brimmed | Do. |
| Kerchief, silk | Crow Village; Weinland. |
| Overalls, bibbed | Crow Village. |
| Overshoes, rubber | Do. |
| Shoes: | |
| High laced (female) | Do. |
| Square toed (male) | Do. |
| Suspenders | Do. |
| Footwear: | |
| Boots: | |
| Hip length (female; rare male); sealskin tops and bottoms. | Informants. |
| Knee length (male): | |
| Caribou skin tops, sealskin bottoms | Do. |
| Fishskin tops and bottoms | Informants; Zagoskin. |
| Boot liners of grass | Do. |
| Socks: | |
| Caribou skin | Do. |
| Fishskin | Informants. |
| Grass, woven | Do. |
| Handwear; mittens or gloves of caribou skin | Do. |
| Headwear: | |
| Cap (male); beaver skin | Informants. |
| Hood; caribou, marten, or squirrel skin | Zagoskin. |
| Leggings | Do. |
| Parka: | |
| Hooded: | |
| Ankle length, split sides (female) | Informants; Zagoskin. |
| Rain parka | Zagoskin. |

APPENDIX TABLE 3.—*Central Kuskokwim Yuk culture, circa 1840–1900*—Continued

| Item | Source |
|---|---|
| Clothing—Continued | |
|   Parka—Continued | |
|     Hoodless: | |
|       Ankle length, sewn sides (male) | Zagoskin. |
|       Knee length (male): | |
|         No trim | Informants. |
|         Trimmed | Do. |
|       Hooded or hoodless; crotch length (male) | Do. |
|     Tobacco bag | Do. |
|     Trousers (male): | |
|       Fitted to below the knees | Do. |
|       Short underpants | Do. |
| Snares; traps; weapons: | |
|   Arrow feathering; two vanes set opposite each other | Informants. |
|   Arrowhead; antler: | |
|     Bilaterally barbed, wedge tang | Do. |
|     Unbarbed, open socket tang | Crow Village. |
|     Unilaterally barbed, wedge tang | Informants. |
|   Arrowhead; wood; blunt | Crow Village. |
|   Beaver hook, iron | Zagoskin. |
|   Bird spear shaft, spruce | Crow Village. |
|   Bow, spruce: | |
|     Sinew backed | Do. |
|     Unbacked | Crow Village; Informants. |
|   Firearms and ammunition: | |
|     Cartridge: | |
|       .44 caliber, rimfire | Crow Village. |
|       .44 caliber, center-fire | Do. |
|       .45–.70 caliber, center-fire | Do. |
|       .22 caliber | Do. |
|     Musket ball | Do. |
|     Percussion cap (container) | Do. |
|     Rifle: | |
|       .44 caliber | Informants. |
|       .45–.70 caliber | Do. |
|     Ramrod, whalebone | Crow Village. |
|   Lance; ground stone point | Do. |
|   Snare: | |
|     Fixed; twisted grass rope | Informants. |
|     Peg | Crow Village. |
|     Spring pole; bird-feather-rib rope | Informants; Zagoskin. |
|   Trap: | |
|     Deadfall | Informants. |
|     Fish trap set for animals | Do. |
|     Netting for trapping land animals | Zagoskin. |
| Subsistence: | |
|   Fish: | |
|     Boiled | Informants; Zagoskin. |
|     Decayed | Do. |
|     Dried | Do. |
|     Smoked | Do. |
|     Frozen | Do. |
|   Meat: | |
|     Boiled | Informants. |
|     Dried | Do. |
|     Roasted | Do. |
|   Tobacco | Zagoskin. |

APPENDIX TABLE 3.—*Central Kuskokwim Yuk culture, circa 1840–1900*—Continued

| Item | Source |
|---|---|
| Subsistence—Continued | |
|   Vegetable: | |
|     Berries: | |
|       Fish eggs, boiled_____ | Informants. |
|       Greens, roots, meat, fish, oil (agutuk)____ | Informants; Zagoskin. |
|       Fireweed, boiled_____ | Informants. |
|       Mushrooms, raw_____ | Do. |
|       Wild rhubarb, boiled_____ | Do. |
| *Kashgee* and Men's Equipment: | |
|   Antler: | |
|     Adz head_____ | Crow Village. |
|     Crooked knife handle_____ | Informants. |
|     Net sinker_____ | Crow Village; Informants. |
|     Wedge_____ | Do. |
|   Bearskin; entrance cover_____ | Informants. |
|   Birchbark: | |
|     Snuffbox sides_____ | Crow Village. |
|     Unworked rolls of birchbark_____ | Do. |
|   Canvas; stage curtain for ceremonies_____ | Informants. |
|   Fur, paintbrush of marmot_____ | Do. |
|   Grass: | |
|     Sponge for bathing_____ | Zagoskin. |
|     Woven for stage curtain for ceremonies____ | Informants; Zagoskin. |
|   Metal: | |
|     Adz blade_____ | Informants. |
|     Awl_____ | Crow Village. |
|     Ax blade_____ | Crow Village; Zagoskin. |
|     Bayonet_____ | Crow Village. |
|     Can metal_____ | Do. |
|     Chisel: | |
|       Brass_____ | Do. |
|       Iron_____ | Do. |
|     Copper sheet_____ | Do. |
|     End blade for knife_____ | Do. |
|     Engraving tool blade_____ | Informants. |
|     Hinge of copper_____ | Crow Village. |
|     Knife_____ | Zagoskin. |
|     Nails_____ | Crow Village. |
|     Saw blade_____ | Do. |
|     Strike-a-light_____ | Do. |
|     Wedge_____ | Do. |
|   Paint: | |
|     Black; coal_____ | Zagoskin. |
|     Blue; white rock and decayed wood_____ | Informants. |
|     Red; blood and ocher_____ | Informants; Zagoskin. |
|     White; white rock_____ | Informants. |
|   Pottery; locally made: | |
|     Lamp; large and bowl shaped_____ | Informants; Zagoskin. |
|   Stone: | |
|     Adz blade: | |
|       Chipped of flinty material_____ | Informants. |
|       Ground: | |
|         Planing_____ | Crow Village. |
|         Splitting_____ | Do. |
|     Bullet mold_____ | Do. |
|     End bladed knife blade_____ | Do. |
|     Grinding stone_____ | Do. |
|     Hammerstone_____ | Do. |
|     Paint mortar_____ | Crow Village; Informants. |

APPENDIX TABLE 3.—*Central Kuskokwim Yuk culture, circa 1840–1900*—Continued

| Item | Source |
|---|---|
| *Kashgee* and Men's Equipment—Continued | |
| Stone—Continued | |
| Saw | Crow Village. |
| Whetstone | Crow Village; Informants. |
| Wood: | |
| Adz handle | Crow Village. |
| Beaver tooth drawknife handle | Do. |
| Crooked knife handle | Informants. |
| Drill shaft: | |
| Bit emplacement | Crow Village. |
| Fire drill | Do. |
| End blade knife handle | Do. |
| Engraving tool handle | Do. |
| Lampstand | Informants. |
| Maul | Crow Village. |
| Paring knife handle | Do. |
| Respirator of shavings | Zagoskin. |
| Snuffbox bottom | Crow Village. |
| Strap drill handle | Do. |
| Tobacco box top and bottom | Do. |
| Wedge | Crow Village; Informants. |
| Ceremonial Life and Equipment: | |
| Burial: | |
| Coffin, plank | Informants. |
| Birchbark over entire coffin | Zagoskin. |
| Birchbark over coffin top | Informants. |
| Corner posts | Informants; Zagoskin. |
| Painted figures on sides | Informants. |
| Figures; free standing, head and trunk | Do. |
| Grave goods: | |
| Tools and equipment (male or female) | Do. |
| Toys (children) | Do. |
| Headboard: | |
| Animal carvings attached | Crow Village; Informants. |
| Human carving attached | Do. |
| Bead adornment (female) | Informants. |
| Ceremonies: | |
| Begging | Do. |
| Boy's hunting | Do. |
| Child's first dance | Do. |
| Doll | Do. |
| Feast for the dead | Do. |
| First salmon | Do. |
| Potlatch | Do. |
| Wild celery stalk | Do. |
| Flower (?) carving | Crow Village. |
| Mask appendage: | |
| Animal carving | Crow Village (?). |
| Boat model | Crow Village. |
| Fish carving | Do. |
| Wand | Do. |
| Face mask: | |
| Bear | Informants. |
| Dog | Zagoskin. |
| Fox | Crow Village. |
| Human | Crow Village; Informants; Zagoskin. |
| Raven | Informants. |
| Spirit | Zagoskin. |

APPENDIX TABLE 3.—*Central Kuskokwim Yuk culture, circa 1840–1900*—Continued

| Item | Source |
|---|---|
| Ceremonial Life and Equipment—Continued | |
| Finger mask_____ | Informants; Zagoskin. |
| Memorial carving of a girl_____ | Informants. |
| Tambourine drum: | |
|     Handle_____ | Crow Village. |
|     Drumstick_____ | Informants. |
| Games: | |
| Ball of twisted grass_____ | Do. |
| Broad jump (males)_____ | Zagoskin. |
| Chopping hole in ice (boys)_____ | Do. |
| Hand game (men)_____ | Informants. |
| Snowshoe race (males)_____ | Zagoskin. |
| Personal Adornment: | |
| Bracelet; copper_____ | Crow Village; Zagoskin. |
| Breast ornament (child, female): | |
|     Beads_____ | Weinland. |
|     Brass buttons_____ | Do. |
| Ear ornament; strung beads, various colors | |
|     (female)_____ | Informants. |
| Labret: | |
| Lateral: | |
|     Disk shaped (male)_____ | Crow Village; Informants. |
|     Hook shaped (female)_____ | Informants. |
|     Ornamented with beads_____ | Informants; Zagoskin. |
|     Medial (male)_____ | Crow Village; Informants. |
| Necklace, beads and cartridge cases (female)_ | Crow Village. |
| Nose ornament, blue glass beads (female)____ | Informants; Zagoskin. |
| Pendant: | |
|     Bear tooth_____ | Crow Village. |
|     Metal_____ | Do. |
| Ring: | |
|     Iron_____ | Zagoskin. |
|     Wire_____ | Do. |
| Tattoo; lip to chin lines (female)_____ | Do. |
| Transportation: | |
| Boats and boating: | |
|     *Bidarra* (umiak)_ _____ | Informants. |
|     Birchbark canoe_____ | Do. |
|     Kayak:_____ | Do. |
|         Bow or stern piece_____ | Crow Village. |
|         Bow piece_____ | Do. |
|         Deck support_____ | Do. |
|         Manhole: | |
|             Ring section_____ | Do. |
|             Ring support_____ | Do. |
|         Rib_____ | Do. |
|     Paddle: | |
|         Double bladed; ribbed on one side of | |
|           blade_____ | Informants. |
|         Incomplete; ribbed on both sides of blade_ | Crow Village. |
|         Single bladed; ribbed on both sides of | |
|           blade_____ | Informants. |
|     Propelling pole_____ | Do. |
| Sled and sledding: | |
|     Built up; flat bed (dog traction)_____ | Do. |
|     Runner: | |
|         Birch_____ | Zagoskin. |
|         Spruce_____ | Crow Village; Informants. |
|     Canoe or kayak sled (human traction)____ | Informants. |
|     Crosspiece_____ | Crow Village. |

APPENDIX TABLE 3.—*Central Kuskokwim Yuk culture, circa 1840–1900*—Continued

| Item | Source |
|---|---|
| Transportation—Continued | |
| Sled and sledding—Continued | |
| Dog harness; old fish net | Informants. |
| Shoe; sled: | |
| Whalebone | Crow Village; Informants. |
| Wood | Crow Village. |
| Stanchion, sled | Do. |
| Snowshoe: | |
| Frame: | |
| Birch | Informants; Zagoskin. |
| Cottonwood | Crow Village. |
| Household Equipment: | |
| Antler; ulu handle | Do. |
| Birchbark: | |
| Basket: | |
| Carrying, large | Informants. |
| Cooking | Do. |
| Household, small | Crow Village; Informants. |
| Horsetail root border design | Informants. |
| Dipper | Do. |
| Plate | Do. |
| Bone; awl | Crow Village. |
| Fishskin; bags | Zagoskin. |
| Flannel; blankets | Do. |
| Glass: | |
| Bottle | Crow Village. |
| Drinking glass | Do. |
| Scraper: | |
| Bottle fragment | Do. |
| Window fragment | Do. |
| Grass: | |
| Woven basket | Informants. |
| Woven | Crow Village. |
| Metal: | |
| Bucket, with handle | Do. |
| Can metal rolls | Do. |
| Dipper | Do. |
| Dish: | |
| Cast iron | Zagoskin. |
| Copper | Do. |
| Remade tin can metal | Crow Village. |
| Frying pan | Do. |
| Ladle | Do. |
| Needle | Zagoskin. |
| Pie tin | Crow Village. |
| Pot | Zagoskin. |
| Pothook | Crow Village. |
| Scraper blade | Do. |
| Tablespoon | Do. |
| Teakettle: | |
| Enameled | Do. |
| Plain metal | Do. |
| Teaspoon | Do. |
| Tin can | Do. |
| Ulu blade from can metal | Do. |
| Moss; lampwick | Informants. |
| Oil; lamp fuel (bear, fish, or seal oil) | Do. |

APPENDIX TABLE 3.—*Central Kuskokwim Yuk culture, circa 1840–1900*—Continued

| Item | Source |
|---|---|
| Household Equipment—Continued | |
| Pottery: | |
| Imported: | |
| Cup: | |
| Hand painted | Crow Village |
| Plain | Do. |
| Transfer print | Do. |
| Saucer | Do. |
| Teapot | Do. |
| Locally made: | |
| Cooking pot: | |
| Line-dot surface treatment | Do. |
| Undecorated | Do. |
| Saucer shaped lamp | Do. |
| Sinew; thread | Zagoskin. |
| Skins; bedding | Informants. |
| Stone: | |
| Dish | Crow Village. |
| Heating stones | Do. |
| Lamp, pecked and ground: | |
| Basin shaped; shallow, wide rim | Do. |
| Bowl shaped, shallow | Do. |
| Scraper: | |
| Flaked: | |
| Boulder chip (tci-tho) | Crow Village. |
| Blade: | |
| End | Do. |
| Side | Do. |
| Ground: | |
| End blade, hafted | Do. |
| Ulu blade | Crow Village; Informants. |
| Tar; lump | Crow Village. |
| Willow; inner bark for nets | Crow Village; Informants; Zagoskin. |
| Wood: | |
| Barrel, imported | Do. |
| Bench support | Do. |
| Bowl, semicircle of a burl | Do. |
| Box, plank, imported | Do. |
| Bucket, ovoid; decorated bottom | Crow Village; Informants. |
| Cup | Informants. |
| Cutting board | Crow Village; Informants. |
| Dish, ovoid | Do. |
| End scraper handle | Do. |
| Food tray, ovoid | Do. |
| Handle | Crow Village. |
| Ladle | Do. |
| Lampstand | Crow Village; Informants. |
| Poke stopper | Crow Village. |
| Ulu handle | Crow Village; Informants. |
| Fishing Equipment: | |
| Fish trap | Informants; Zagoskin. |
| Harpoon dart; barbed metal point | Crow Village. |
| Hook and line: | |
| Hook baited with red flannel | Informants. |
| Rod | Crow Village; Informants. |
| Leister: | |
| Central prong | Crow Village. |
| Lateral prong | Do. |

APPENDIX TABLE 3.—*Central Kuskokwim Yuk culture, circa 1840–1900*—Continued

| Item | Source |
|------|--------|
| Fishing Equipment—Continued | |
| Net: | |
| Dip net | Informants; Zagoskin. |
| Gill net | Do. |
| Drift | Do. |
| Set | Informants. |
| Material: | |
| Cotton twine | Do. |
| Rawhide thong | Informants; Zagoskin. |
| Twisted grass | Informants. |
| Willow inner bark | Crow Village; Informants; Zagoskin. |
| Netting equipment: | |
| Anchor stone | Informants. |
| Anchor lines of willow inner bark | Do. |
| Fish killing: | |
| Awl | Do. |
| Club | Do. |
| Float: | |
| Oblong with holes at each end: | |
| Cottonwood bark | Crow Village; Zagoskin. |
| Spruce | Crow Village. |
| Oblong with hole at one end; spruce | Crow Village; Informants. |
| Shaped like duck, for end of drift net | Informants. |
| Gage | Crow Village; Informants. |
| Net container for boat | Informants. |
| Shuttle | Crow Village; Informants. |
| Weight: | |
| Antler, drilled holes | Do. |
| Bone, notched | Crow Village. |
| Lead, clamped | Informants. |
| Stone, notched | Crow Village. |
| Weir | Informants; Zagoskin. |

# INDEX

○